Robert Rose's Favorite
MEALS IN MINUTES

ROBERT ROSE'S FAVORITE MEALS IN MINUTES

Canadian Cataloguing in Publication Data

Main entry under title:

Robert Rose's favorite meals in minutes

Includes index.

ISBN 0-7788-0008-3

1. Quick and easy cookery.   I. Title: Meals in minutes.

TX833.5R63 1999   641.5'55   C99-930002-4

DESIGN, EDITORIAL AND PRODUCTION: MATTHEWS COMMUNICATIONS DESIGN INC.
PHOTOGRAPHY: MARK T. SHAPIRO

Cover photo: (MAMA'S ITALIAN CHEESEBURGERS, PAGE 43)

We acknowledge the financial support of the Government of Canada through the Book Publishing Industry Development Program (BPIDP) for our publishing activities.

Canada

Published by: Robert Rose Inc. • 156 Duncan Mill Road, Suite 12
Toronto, Ontario, Canada M3B 2N2   Tel: (416) 449-3535

Printed in Canada   1234567 BP 02 01 00 99

About this book

At Robert Rose, we're committed to finding imaginative and exciting ways to provide our readers with cookbooks that offer great recipes — and exceptional value. That's the thinking behind our "Robert Rose's Favorite" series.

Here we've selected over 50 favorite ready-in-minutes recipes from a number of our bestselling full-sized cookbooks: Byron Ayanoglu's *New Vegetarian Gourmet* and *Simply Mediterranean Cooking*; Johanna Burkhard's *Comfort Food Cookbook* and *Fast & Easy Cooking*; Andrew Chase's *Asian Bistro Cookbook*; Cinda Chavich's *Wild West Cookbook*; *New World Noodles* and *New World Chinese Cooking*, by Bill Jones and Stephen Wong; Kathleen Sloan's *Rustic Italian Cooking* and Rose Reisman's *Light Cooking, Light Pasta, Enlightened Home Cooking* and *Light Vegetarian Cooking*.

We believe that it all adds up to great value for anyone who loves good food — fast.

Want to find out more about the series? See page 96.

Contents

Appetizers

Greek Chicken Pita Sandwiches 7
Bitter Greens with Paprika 8
Brie-Stuffed Mushrooms 9
Crab and Corn Pancakes with Sweet-and-Sour Sauce 10
Beyond Bean Dip 12
Ricotta and Smoked Salmon Tortilla Bites 14
Shrimp and Snow Pea Tidbits 15
Tuscan Garlic Tomato Bread 16
Mini Pesto Shrimp Tortilla Pizzas 19
Antipasto Nibblers 20

Soups & Salads

Tortellini Minestrone with Spinach 23
Vietnamese-Style Beef Noodle Soup 24
Cheddar Broccoli Chowder 25
Cauliflower and White Bean Soup 26
Ramen Noodle Soup with a Tangy Tomato and Sweet Corn Broth 27
Green Bean and Plum Tomato Salad 29
Summer Artichoke Salad 30
Thai Beef Salad 32

Main Dishes

Indian-Style Grilled Chicken Breasts 35
Chicken with Fig and Orange Sauce 36
Chinese Lemon Chicken on a Bed of
Red Peppers and Snow Peas 37
Black Bean, Corn and Leek Frittata 38
Chicken Breasts Stuffed with Brie Cheese, Red Pepper and Green Onions 40
Thick Rice Noodles with a Beef, Onion, Corn and Rosemary Sauce 41
Mama's Italian Cheeseburgers 43
Veal Paprikash 44
Four-Cheese Macaroni 45
Simply Super Salmon with Lemon-Oregano Pesto 46
Swordfish with Mango Coriander Salsa 49
Salmon over White-and-Black-Bean Salsa 50
Linguine with Caramelized Onions, Tomatoes and Basil 53
Rotini Alfredo with Asparagus, Sweet Red Pepper and Prosciutto 54

Vegetables and Side Dishes

Rapini with Balsamic Vinegar 57
Lemon-Glazed Baby Carrots 58
Cheese and Red Pepper Stuffed Potatoes 59
Spicy Rice with Feta Cheese and Black Olives 60
Piedmont Peppers 63
Jalapeno Broccoli 64
Roasted Garlic Sweet Pepper Strips 65
Green Beans with Cashews 67
Asparagus, Red Pepper and Goat Cheese Phyllo Roll 69
Mushrooms with Creamy Feta Cheese and Dill Stuffing 70
Sugar Snap Peas with Sesame Sauce 71
Eggplant with Goat Cheese and Roasted Sweet Peppers 72
Cheese and Salsa Quesadillas 73
Herbed Potatoes 74

Desserts

Farmhouse Apple Pie 77
Lemon Poppy Seed Squares 78
Blueberry Banana Muffins 79
Lemon Fool with Fresh Berries 80
Baked Pears 83
Chocolate Fondue 84
Mocha Brownies with Cream Cheese Icing 85
Cream Cheese-Filled Brownies 86
Fried Pineapple 89
Candied Ginger and Strawberry Parfait 90
Peanutty Cereal Snacking Bars 91
Baked Wontons Stuffed with Apples and Cinnamon 92

Index 93

Appetizers

Greek Chicken Pita Sandwiches

When I'm in the mood for something easy for dinner, this is what I make. It beats sandwiches or burgers from fast food restaurants hands down.

TIP

A combination of lemon juice, garlic and oregano is the classic marinade for souvlaki. I also use it as a quick marinade combined with 1 tbsp (15 mL) olive oil to brush-over chicken breasts and pork loin chops on the barbecue.

1 lb	skinless, boneless chicken breasts, cut into very thin strips	500 g
1 tbsp	freshly squeezed lemon juice	15 mL
1	large clove garlic, minced	1
3/4 tsp	dried oregano	4 mL
1/4 tsp	salt	1 mL
1/4 tsp	pepper	1 mL
2 tsp	olive oil	10 mL
1	small red onion, halved lengthwise and thinly sliced	1
1	red or green bell pepper, cut into 2-inch (5 cm) thin strips	1
4	pitas (7-inch [18 cm] size), halved to make pockets	4
3/4 cup	tzatziki sauce	175 mL
4 cups	shredded romaine lettuce	1 L
2	tomatoes, cut into wedges	2

1. In a bowl, combine chicken, lemon juice, garlic, oregano, salt and pepper. Marinate at room temperature for 10 minutes.

2. In a large nonstick skillet, heat oil over high heat; cook chicken, stirring, for 2 to 3 minutes or until no longer pink. Add onion and bell pepper; cook, stirring, for 2 minutes or until vegetables are softened.

3. Wrap pitas in paper towels; microwave at Medium for 1 1/2 minutes or until warm. Spoon chicken mixture into pita halves; top with a generous spoonful of tzatziki sauce, shredded lettuce and tomato wedges.

FROM
Fast & Easy Cooking
by Johanna Burkhard

Bitter Greens with Paprika

Serves 3 or 4

Suitable as a starter or as a side dish with grilled or roasted meat, this hyper-nutritious dish has taste to spare. Here the bitterness of the main ingredient merges meaningfully with the various aromatics and condiments. A whole new dimension can be achieved by using non-bitter greens — like collard or kale — with exactly the same enhancements, making this an all-season recipe for the greens of your choice.

1	bunch rapini *or* dandelion greens, washed, bottom 2 inches (5 cm) of stalks trimmed	1
2 tbsp	olive oil	25 mL
1 tsp	sweet paprika	5 mL
1/4 tsp	turmeric	1 mL
1/4 tsp	salt	1 mL
1/4 tsp	freshly ground black pepper	1 mL
3	cloves garlic, thinly sliced	3
2 tbsp	lemon juice	25 mL
1 tsp	drained capers	5 mL

1. Cut the stalks of the greens in half. Bring a pot of salted water to a boil and add the lower half of the stalks. Let the water return to a boil and cook for 3 minutes. Add the upper half of the stalks (with the leaves); return to a boil and cook for 3 minutes. Rinse under cold water; drain and set aside.

2. In a large frying pan, combine oil, paprika, turmeric, salt and pepper. Cook, stirring, over high heat for 1 minute. Add garlic; stir-fry for 30 seconds. Add drained greens; stir-fry for 2 minutes, folding from the bottom up to distribute garlic and spices evenly. Reduce the heat to medium. Stir in lemon juice; cook, stirring, for 2 minutes. Stir in capers. Serve immediately.

FROM
Simply Mediterranean Cooking by Byron Ayanoglu & Algis Kemezys

FROM
Rose Reisman's
Light Vegetarian Cooking

Brie-Stuffed Mushrooms

Serves 4

TIP

Don't throw out those mushroom stems — use them in salads or soups, or sauté in a nonstick skillet and serve as a side vegetable dish.

Roast your own red bell peppers or buy water-packed roasted red peppers.

Use another soft cheese of your choice to replace the Brie.

MAKE AHEAD

Fill mushroom caps up to 1 day in advance. Bake just before serving.

PREHEAT OVEN TO 400° F (200° C)
BAKING SHEET

16 to 20	medium mushrooms	16 to 20
2 oz	Brie cheese	50 g
1/4 cup	chopped roasted red peppers	50 mL
1/4 cup	chopped green onions	50 mL
3 tbsp	dried bread crumbs	45 mL
1 tsp	minced garlic	5 mL
1/2 tsp	dried basil	2 mL

1. Wipe mushrooms; remove stems and reserve for another use. (See Tip, at left.) Place on the baking sheet.

2. In a small bowl, stir together Brie, red peppers, green onions, bread crumbs, garlic and basil. Divide mixture among mushroom caps, approximately 1 1/2 tsp (7 mL) per cap.

3. Bake for 15 minutes, or until mushrooms release their liquid. Serve warm or at room temperature.

Crab and Corn Pancakes with Sweet-and-Sour Sauce

Pancakes make versatile appetizers. This version marries a Chinese sweet-and-sour sauce with a New England-style corn and crabcake. The combination of butter and oil for frying helps to achieve a rich, golden brown finish.

PREHEAT OVEN TO WARM

Sauce

1 cup	tomato juice	250 mL
2 tbsp	brown sugar	25 mL
2 tbsp	rice vinegar	25 mL
1 tbsp	minced ginger root	15 mL
1 tbsp	grated horseradish	15 mL
1 tsp	cornstarch dissolved in 2 tbsp (25 mL) cold water	5 mL
1 tbsp	chopped cilantro	15 mL

Pancakes

4 oz	fresh or canned crab meat	125 g
1 cup	fresh or frozen corn kernels	250 mL
2	large eggs, lightly beaten	2
2 tbsp	cream *or* milk	25 mL
6 tbsp	all-purpose flour	90 mL
2 tsp	baking powder	10 mL
	Salt and pepper to taste	
1 tbsp	vegetable oil	15 mL
1 tbsp	butter	15 mL

1. In a small saucepan over medium-high heat, combine tomato juice, brown sugar, rice vinegar, ginger root and horseradish. Reduce heat to simmer; add dissolved cornstarch and stir until thickened. Add cilantro; mix well. Remove from heat and set aside.

2. In a mixing bowl, combine crab and corn. Add eggs, cream (or milk), flour and baking powder. Season to taste with salt and pepper. Mix well.

3. In a nonstick skillet, heat oil and butter over medium-high heat. Spoon batter into the pan to make 4 pancakes, each 2 inches (5 cm) in diameter. Cook 2 to 3 minutes per side or until golden. Keep warm. Repeat cooking procedure until all the batter is used up. Serve warm topped with sauce.

FROM
New World Chinese Cooking
by Bill Jones and Stephen Wong

**Makes about
7 cups (1.75 L)**

Although the texture of canned beans is inferior for dishes that call for whole beans, they are simple and fast to use — especially for dips or refried bean dishes. Rinse and drain canned beans before using.

Beyond Bean Dip

Bean layer

1	can (14 oz [398 mL]) refried beans *or* 1 can (19 oz [540 mL]) pinto beans	1
1/4 cup	sour cream	50 mL
1	jalapeno pepper, seeded and minced	1
1	clove garlic, minced	1
1 tsp	chili powder	5 mL
1/2 tsp	ground cumin	2 mL

Guacamole layer

2	ripe avocados	2
3 tbsp	lemon juice *or* lime juice	45 mL
3	green onions, minced	3
1 tsp	minced jalapeno pepper	5 mL

Garnish

1 cup	sour cream	250 mL
2	green onions, chopped	2
1	tomato, seeded and chopped	1
1 cup	shredded Cheddar cheese	250 mL
1/2 cup	sliced black olives	125 mL
	Regular and blue corn tortilla chips as accompaniments	

1. If using pinto beans, rinse and drain. Purée beans in a food processor; transfer to a bowl. Stir in sour cream, jalapeno, garlic, chili powder and cumin. Set aside.

2. In another bowl, mash avocados with lemon juice. Stir in green onions and jalapeno peppers. Set aside.

3. Spread the bean dip in a thin layer over a deep 12-inch (30 cm) platter. Carefully spread guacamole over bean layer. Spread with sour cream, making sure to cover guacamole completely to keep it from darkening. Starting at the outside edge of the plate, make a 2-inch (5 cm) ring of shredded cheese. Inside that ring, sprinkle green onions in a ring. Follow with black olives and finish with a pile of chopped tomato in the center of the plate. Serve with lots of regular and blue corn tortilla chips for scooping.

**FROM
The Wild West Cookbook
by Cinda Chavich**

Ricotta and Smoked Salmon Tortilla Bites

TIP

These are best served at room temperature.

MAKE AHEAD

Make early in the day and refrigerate. Arrange on a lettuce-lined plate just before serving.

1 cup	ricotta cheese	250 mL
1 tbsp	light mayonnaise *or* light sour cream	15 mL
2 tbsp	chopped fresh dill (or 1/2 tsp [2 mL] dried)	25 mL
2 tbsp	finely chopped chives *or* green onions	25 mL
2 oz	smoked salmon, diced	50 g
4	flour tortillas	4
	Lettuce leaves	

1. In a bowl or food processor, combine ricotta and light mayonnaise until smooth. Gently stir in dill, chives and smoked salmon until combined.

2. Divide filling among the tortillas, spreading evenly. Roll up jelly roll style. Cut each tortilla into 6 pieces. Arrange on a lettuce-lined plate.

**FROM
Rose Reisman Brings Home
Light Cooking**

Serves 4 to 6
or makes 16
hors d'oeuvres

TIP

Buy snow peas that are firm and crisp, and have no blemishes.

•

Medium-sized scallops would also be delicious for this very sophisticated hors d'oeuvre.

MAKE AHEAD

If serving cold, prepare and refrigerate early in the day.

FROM
**Rose Reisman Brings Home
Light Cooking**

Shrimp and Snow Pea Tidbits

16	snow peas	16
2 tsp	vegetable oil	10 mL
1 tsp	crushed garlic	5 mL
1 tbsp	chopped fresh parsley	15 mL
16	medium shrimp, peeled, deveined, tail left on	16

1. Steam or microwave the snow peas until they are barely tender-crisp. Rinse with cold water. Drain and set aside.

2. In a nonstick skillet, heat oil; sauté garlic, parsley and shrimp just until the shrimp turn pink, for about 3 to 5 minutes.

3. Wrap each snow pea around shrimp; fasten with a toothpick. Serve warm or cold.

Tuscan Garlic Tomato Bread

Serves 6

Fett'unta and bruschetta are much the same, each based on good country-style bread, sliced and grilled or toasted. Here we find the essence of rustic Italian eating — something that could only have been conceived in a country with such an abiding love for olive oil and tomatoes.

If you can toast the bread over a wood-burning fire, so much the better. And don't even think of making this Tuscan specialty with anything other than the ripest, heftiest plum tomatoes. Try to use an olive oil with a green, peppery quality. This recipe is easily doubled or tripled.

3	large ripe plum tomatoes	3
6	thick slices of rustic country-style bread	6
3	large cloves garlic, peeled and cut in half	3
1/4 cup	extra virgin olive oil	50 mL
	Salt and freshly ground black pepper to taste	

1. Cut the tomatoes in half and squeeze to remove seeds and juice.

2. Toast or grill the bread until lightly browned. Rub one side of each bread slice with half a clove of garlic. Then roughly rub a deseeded tomato half over the same side of the bread until the bread begins to take on the color and the essence of the tomato. Repeat procedure with remaining bread, garlic and tomato.

3. Place bread on a serving platter. Drizzle with the olive oil and season each slice with salt and pepper.

**FROM
Rustic Italian Cooking
by Kathleen Sloan**

FROM
**Rose Reisman's Enlightened
Home Cooking**

Mini Pesto Shrimp Tortilla Pizzas

Serves 8

TIP

Two large tortillas can be used instead of the 4 small ones.

•

Any vegetables or other cheese, such as goat cheese, can be substituted.

MAKE AHEAD

Prepare the pizzas early in the day. Keep covered and refrigerated until ready to bake.

•

Pizzas can also be prepared and frozen for up to 6 weeks.

PREHEAT OVEN TO 400° F (200° C)
BAKING SHEET SPRAYED WITH VEGETABLE SPRAY

4	small flour tortillas	4
1/3 cup	pesto	75 mL
1/2 cup	finely chopped red peppers	125 mL
1/2 cup	finely chopped cooked shrimp	125 mL
2/3 cup	shredded part-skim mozzarella cheese	150 mL

1. Place tortillas on the baking sheet. Divide pesto among the tortillas; spread evenly.

2. Top the tortillas with red peppers, shrimp and mozzarella.

3. Bake for 12 to 15 minutes or until cheese melts and the tortillas are crisp. Cut each into 4 pieces.

Antipasto Nibblers

Here's another last-minute idea for tasty bites to serve when friends drop over. These small nibblers are a throwback to the cocktail/lounge scene of the 1960s, when appetizers often meant cold cuts wrapped around a pickle. I like them because they can be assembled in a few minutes and are a colorful addition to a tray of warm appetizers.

TIP

This recipe can be varied according to what you have on hand. Thin slices of salami or ham folded in half, cocktail onions and marinated artichoke pieces make for other easy combinations.

24	stuffed green olives *or* Kalamata olives	24
8 oz	Fontina cheese, cut into 3/4-inch (2 cm) cubes	250 g
1	small sweet red pepper, cut into 1-inch (2.5 cm) squares	1
1	small sweet green pepper, cut into 1-inch (2.5 cm) squares	1
1 tbsp	olive oil	15 mL
1 tbsp	balsamic vinegar	15 mL
	Pepper	
2 tbsp	chopped fresh basil *or* parsley	25 mL

1. Thread 1 olive, 1 cheese cube and then 1 pepper square onto cocktail toothpicks. Arrange in an attractive shallow serving dish. Cover and refrigerate until serving time.

2. In a small bowl, whisk together oil and balsamic vinegar; pour over kabobs. Season generously with pepper; sprinkle with basil and serve.

FROM
The Comfort Food Cookbook
by Johanna Burkhard

Soups & Salads

Serves 4 to 6

TIP

Try ravioli or gnocchi instead of tortellini.

•

If fresh spinach is unavailable, substitute 1/4 of a 10-oz (300 g) package of frozen spinach. Thaw and drain the excess liquid.

•

Plum tomatoes can be replaced with the regular variety.

MAKE AHEAD

Prepare the soup up to 2 days in advance, but do not add tortellini until ready to re-heat and serve.

•

Can be frozen for up to 3 weeks.

FROM
Rose Reisman's
Light Vegetarian Cooking

Tortellini Minestrone with Spinach

2 tsp	vegetable oil	10 mL
2 tsp	minced garlic	10 mL
1 cup	chopped onions	250 mL
1/2 cup	chopped carrots	125 mL
1/2 cup	chopped celery	125 mL
4 cups	vegetable stock	1 L
1 tsp	dried basil	5 mL
1/4 tsp	freshly ground black pepper	1 mL
1 1/2 cups	diced plum tomatoes	375 mL
2 cups	chopped fresh spinach	500 mL
2 cups	frozen cheese tortellini	500 mL
3 tbsp	grated Parmesan cheese	45 mL

1. In a nonstick saucepan sprayed with vegetable spray, heat oil over medium–high heat. Add garlic, onions, carrots and celery; cook for 4 minutes or until the onions are softened.

2. Add stock, basil and pepper. Bring to a boil; reduce heat to medium and cook for 8 minutes or until the vegetables are tender-crisp.

3. Stir in tomatoes, spinach and tortellini. Cover and cook for 5 minutes or until the tortellini is heated through and the vegetables are tender. Serve immediately, garnished with Parmesan cheese.

Vietnamese-Style Beef Noodle Soup

A variation on the famous Vietnamese *Pho*, this is a great way to use up leftover roasts, including pork or lamb.

8 oz	thin vermicelli (thin rice stick) noodles *or* dried angel hair pasta Vegetable oil for coating noodles	250 g

Broth

6 cups	beef stock	1.5 L
1	stalk lemon grass, smashed and cut into 4-inch (10 cm) lengths *or* 1 tbsp (15 mL) lemon zest	1
3	slices ginger root, smashed	3
1/2 tsp	5-spice powder (optional)	2 mL
1	small onion, thinly sliced	1
1	clove garlic, thinly sliced	1
1 tbsp	fish sauce	15 mL
	Freshly ground black pepper, to taste	
2 cups	bean sprouts	500 mL
1 cup	watercress leaves (optional)	250 mL
12 oz	thinly sliced roast beef	375 g
2 tbsp	thinly sliced fresh basil leaves	25 mL
1 or 2	red chilies, thinly sliced crosswise	1 or 2
1	lime, quartered	1

1. In a heatproof bowl or pot, cover noodles with boiling water and soak for 3 minutes. (If using pasta, prepare according to the package directions.) Drain, coat with a little oil and set aside.

2. In a large saucepan, bring stock to a boil. Add lemon grass, ginger root and 5-spice powder (if using); reduce heat to medium; cover and cook for 3 minutes.

3. With a slotted spoon, remove lemon grass and ginger root. Add onion and garlic; bring to a boil and cook for 1 minute. Season with fish sauce and pepper.

4. Meanwhile, divide noodles into 4 large soup bowls. Top each with one quarter of the bean sprouts, the watercress leaves and the beef slices. Garnish with basil and chilies. Pour boiling broth over noodle mixture and serve with wedges of lime to squeeze over soup.

FROM
New World Noodles
by Bill Jones and Stephen Wong

Cheddar Broccoli Chowder

Serves 6

My vegetarian daughter loves this soup and so do I. It's no fuss to prepare, easy to reheat and makes a complete meal. With a vegetarian in the family, this is a recipe I count on.

TIP

Depending on what I have in the fridge, I make variations on this versatile, tasty soup by using other vegetables, such as carrots and cauliflower.

2 tbsp	butter	25 mL
1	small onion, finely chopped	1
1/4 cup	all-purpose flour	50 mL
3 cups	vegetable stock *or* chicken stock	750 mL
2 cups	potatoes, peeled and cut into 1/2-inch (1 cm) cubes	500 mL
1	bay leaf	1
3 cups	finely chopped broccoli florets and peeled stalks	750 mL
1 1/2 cups	milk	375 mL
1 1/2 cups	shredded Cheddar cheese	375 mL
	Pepper	

1. Melt butter in a large saucepan over medium heat. Cook onion, stirring, for 2 minutes or until softened. Blend in flour; stir in stock. Bring to a boil, stirring, until thickened.

2. Add potatoes and bay leaf; reduce heat, cover and simmer, stirring occasionally, for 10 minutes.

3. Add broccoli; simmer, stirring occasionally, for 10 minutes more or until the vegetables are tender.

4. Stir in milk and cheese; heat just until cheese melts and the soup is piping hot. Do not let the soup boil or it may curdle. Remove bay leaf; adjust seasoning with pepper to taste.

FROM
The Comfort Food Cookbook
by Johanna Burkhard

Cauliflower and White Bean Soup

1 tsp	vegetable oil	5 mL
1 tsp	minced garlic	5 mL
1 cup	chopped onions	250 mL
3 2/3 cups	chicken stock	900 mL
3 cups	cauliflower florets	750 mL
1 1/2 cups	canned white kidney beans, drained	375 mL
1 cup	peeled diced potatoes	250 mL
1/4 tsp	ground black pepper	1 mL
1/4 cup	chopped fresh dill (or 1 tsp [5 mL] dried)	50 mL
2 tbsp	chopped chives *or* green onions	25 mL

1. In a nonstick saucepan sprayed with vegetable spray, heat oil over medium heat. Add garlic and onions; cook for 4 minutes or until softened. Add stock, cauliflower, kidney beans, potatoes, pepper and dried dill, if using; bring to a boil. Cover, reduce heat to low and simmer for 20 to 25 minutes or until the vegetables are tender.

2. Transfer the soup to a food processor or blender; purée. Serve garnished with fresh dill, if using, and chives.

FROM
Rose Reisman's Enlightened
Home Cooking

Serves 2 to 4

This makes a quick and delicious meal.

•

If you're using stock, discard the flavor packets that usually come with ramen noodles — they're often heavily seasoned with salt and MSG and, in combination with stock, they will be overpowering.

Ramen Noodle Soup with a Tangy Tomato and Sweet Corn Broth

4 cups	water *or* chicken stock	1 L
2 tbsp	tomato ketchup	25 mL
1 tbsp	*char sui* sauce *or* barbecue sauce	15 mL
1 tbsp	rice vinegar	15 mL
1 tsp	hot sauce, such as Tabasco	5 mL
1 tbsp	minced garlic	15 mL
2	packages ramen noodles, with optional seasoning	2
1 cup	fresh or frozen corn kernels	250 mL
1 tbsp	cornstarch, dissolved in 2 tbsp (25 mL) water	15 mL
	Salt and pepper to taste	
1 tbsp	minced cilantro	15 mL

1. In a large saucepan, bring water or stock to a boil. Add ketchup, *char sui* or barbecue sauce, rice vinegar, hot sauce and garlic. Bring to a boil; add noodles and corn. Reduce heat to simmer and cook for 3 minutes or until noodles are soft.

2. Add seasoning packet to taste, if using. Add dissolved cornstarch. Return to a boil; cook, stirring, until mixture thickens. Season to taste with salt and pepper. Garnish with cilantro and serve immediately.

FROM
New World Chinese Cooking
by Bill Jones and Stephen Wong

Serves 6

When preparing this dish ahead, I like to keep the blanched green beans, tomatoes and dressing separate and toss them just before serving to prevent the salad from getting soggy.

TIP

Use the terrific mustardy dressing with other favorite vegetable salad mixtures and crisp greens.

Green Bean and Plum Tomato Salad

Dressing

1/4 cup	olive oil	50 mL
4 tsp	red wine vinegar	20 mL
1 tbsp	grainy mustard	15 mL
1	clove garlic, minced	1
1/2 tsp	granulated sugar	2 mL
1/4 tsp	salt	1 mL
1/4 tsp	pepper	1 mL
1/4 cup	chopped parsley	50 mL

Salad

1 lb	young green beans, trimmed	500 g
8	small plum tomatoes (about 1 lb [500 g])	8
2	green onions, chopped	2

1. Dressing: In a small bowl, whisk together oil, vinegar, mustard, garlic, sugar, salt and pepper. Stir in parsley.

2. Salad: Cook beans in a medium saucepan of boiling salted water for 3 to 5 minutes or until just tender-crisp. Drain and rinse under cold water to chill; drain well. Pat dry with paper towels or wrap in a clean, dry towel. Cut plum tomatoes in half lengthwise; using a small spoon, scoop out the centers. Cut each piece again in half lengthwise; place in a bowl.

3. Just before serving, combine beans, tomatoes and green onions in a serving bowl. Pour dressing over and toss well.

FROM
Fast & Easy Cooking
by Johanna Burkhard

Summer Artichoke Salad

Serves 4

Baby artichokes are a gift of nature. Here we find all the glory of grown-up artichokes, but with an edible choke (the fuzz that grows out and protects the heart) — which means zero work and all pleasure. Even more to the point, baby artichokes come to us already cooked (well, a bit overcooked) and ready to use. They're available bottled in oil or canned in water. If using ready-made, I recommend the canned. If using fresh, remove the outer leaves, cut 1/2 inch (1 cm) off the top, trim the stalk and boil over medium heat for 15 minutes until the hearts (bottoms) are easily pierced.

6	baby artichokes, cooked *or* 14-oz (398 mL) can artichoke hearts, rinsed and drained	6
Half	red bell pepper, cut into thin strips	Half
1/4 cup	thinly sliced red onions	50 mL
1	1-inch (2.5 cm) piece English cucumber, thinly sliced	1
5	black olives, pitted and halved	5
1	ripe large tomato, cut into 1/2-inch (1 cm) wedges	1
12	seedless grapes, halved	12
1 tsp	drained capers	5 mL
1	clove garlic, pressed	1
2 tbsp	extra virgin olive oil	25 mL
1 tbsp	white wine vinegar	15 mL
1 tbsp	lemon juice	15 mL
1/4 tsp	salt	1 mL
1/8 tsp	freshly ground black pepper	0.5 mL
	Few sprigs fresh parsley, chopped	

1. Cut the artichokes in half and put in a salad bowl. Add red pepper, onions, cucumber, olives, tomato, grapes and capers. Toss gently to mix.

2. In a small bowl, whisk together garlic, olive oil, vinegar, lemon juice, salt and pepper until slightly emulsified. Drizzle over the salad and toss gently to dress all the pieces, but without breaking up the artichokes too much. Garnish with parsley, and serve within 1 hour (cover if it has to wait, but do not refrigerate).

FROM
Simply Mediterranean Cooking by Byron Ayanoglu & Algis Kemezys

Serves 6

Thai Beef Salad

TIP

Use a good-quality steak such as rib eye, sirloin or porterhouse.

•

You can use leftover roast beef or cooked steak.

•

Chicken or pork can replace steak.

•

Dressing is great for other salads.

MAKE AHEAD

Prepare dressing up to 2 days in advance. Toss just before serving.

8 oz	boneless steak, sliced thinly	250 g
1 3/4 cups	halved snow peas	425 mL
5 cups	well-packed romaine lettuce, washed, dried and torn into bite-size pieces	1.25 L
1 cup	chopped cucumber	250 mL
3/4 cup	sliced red onions	175 mL
3/4 cup	sliced water chestnuts	175 mL
3/4 cup	canned mandarin oranges, drained	175 mL
1	medium red pepper, sliced	1

Dressing

1 1/2 tbsp	orange juice concentrate, thawed	20 mL
4 tsp	honey	20 mL
1 tbsp	rice wine vinegar	15 mL
1 tbsp	soya sauce	15 mL
2 tsp	vegetable oil	10 mL
2 tsp	sesame oil	10 mL
1 tsp	minced garlic	5 mL
3/4 tsp	minced ginger root	4 mL
1/2 tsp	grated orange zest	2 mL

1. In nonstick skillet sprayed with vegetable spray, cook beef over high heat for 90 seconds or until just done at center. Drain any excess liquid. Put in large serving bowl.

2. In a saucepan of boiling water or microwave, blanch snow peas for 1 or 2 minutes, or until tender-crisp; refresh in cold water and drain. Place in serving bowl, along with lettuce, cucumber, red onions, water chestnuts, mandarin oranges and red pepper.

3. In a small bowl, whisk together orange juice concentrate, honey, vinegar, soya sauce, vegetable oil, sesame oil, garlic, ginger and orange zest; pour over salad and toss well.

FROM
Rose Reisman's Enlightened
Home Cooking

Main Dishes

Ginger, cumin, coriander and cayenne pepper are signature ingredients in Indian cooking. Not only do they make chicken taste wonderful, but I love the way the spicy yogurt marinade keeps it moist and tender.

TIP

If you have time, let the chicken marinate for several hours or overnight in the refrigerator to intensify the flavors. To avoid bacterial contamination, baste the chicken only once halfway through cooking, then discard any leftover marinade.

FROM
Fast & Easy Cooking
by Johanna Burkhard

Indian-Style Grilled Chicken Breasts

PREHEAT BARBECUE GRILL TO MEDIUM-HIGH OR OVEN TO 350° F (180° C)
GREASED BARBECUE GRILL OR GREASED BAKING SHEET WITH RACK

1/2 cup	plain low-fat yogurt	125 mL
1 tbsp	tomato paste	15 mL
2	green onions, coarsely chopped	2
2	cloves garlic, quartered	2
1	piece (1-inch [2.5 cm]) peeled ginger root, coarsely chopped (*or* 1 tsp [5 mL] ground ginger)	1
1/2 tsp	ground cumin	2 mL
1/2 tsp	ground coriander	2 mL
1/2 tsp	salt	2 mL
1/4 tsp	cayenne pepper	1 mL
4	chicken breasts (bone-in)	4
2 tbsp	chopped fresh coriander *or* parsley	25 mL

1. In a food processor, combine yogurt, tomato paste, green onions, garlic, ginger, cumin, coriander, salt and cayenne pepper; purée until smooth.

2. Arrange chicken in a shallow dish; coat with yogurt mixture. Cover and refrigerate for 1 hour or up to 1 day ahead. Remove from the refrigerator 30 minutes before cooking.

3. Place the chicken skin-side down on prepared grill; cook for 15 minutes. Brush with marinade; turn and cook for 10 to 15 minutes longer or until golden and juices run clear. (Or place chicken on rack set on baking sheet; roast, basting after 30 minutes with marinade, for 50 to 55 minutes or until juices run clear.) Serve garnished with chopped coriander.

Chicken with Fig and Orange Sauce

Serves 2 or 3

Here's a dish that resulted from our experiments in combining the flavors of dried figs, balsamic vinegar and orange juice to come up with something "new." Of course, nothing new is worth having unless it speaks of and improves upon the old. We hope you'll agree that this chicken dish — with its subtle counterpoints of sweet, tart and spicy—is not only delicious, but very much in line with its culinary precursors from France and Italy.

8 oz	skinless boneless chicken breast cut into 1/2-inch (1 cm) strips	250 g
2 tbsp	all-purpose flour	25 mL
2 tbsp	olive oil	25 mL
1/2 tsp	fennel seeds	2 mL
1/4 tsp	freshly ground black pepper	1 mL
1	onion, thinly sliced	1
1	dried fig, thinly sliced	1
1 tsp	balsamic vinegar	5 mL
1 cup	orange juice	250 mL
1/2 cup	white wine	125 mL
	Salt to taste	
	Steamed rice as an accompaniment	
2	green onions, finely chopped	2

1. Lightly dredge the chicken in the flour and set aside.

2. In a large nonstick frying pan, heat oil with the fennel seeds and pepper over high heat for 1 minute. Add onion and fig; stir-fry for 2 minutes or until softened. Add balsamic vinegar; cook, stirring, for 30 seconds or until absorbed.

3. Immediately add chicken; stir-fry actively for 2 minutes or until chicken is lightly browned. (Be sure to avoid burning figs and onions.) Add orange juice and bring to a boil. Add wine and cook, stirring, for 1 to 2 minutes or until the sauce becomes syrupy. Season to taste with salt. Remove from heat.

4. Arrange on plates alongside steamed rice and pour sauce over everything. Serve garnished with chopped green onions.

FROM
Simply Mediterranean Cooking by
Byron Ayanoglu & Algis Kemezys

Chinese Lemon Chicken on a Bed of Red Peppers and Snow Peas

Serves 4

TIP

This is a beautiful looking dish. If you substitute any vegetables, try to keep contrasting colors.

•

Replace chicken with turkey, veal or pork scallopini.

MAKE AHEAD

Prepare the sauce earlier in the day. Add a little water if too thick before serving.

FROM
Rose Reisman's Enlightened
Home Cooking

1 tsp	vegetable oil	5 mL
1 1/2 cups	thinly sliced red bell peppers	375 mL
1 1/2 cups	sugar snap peas *or* halved snow peas	375 mL
1 lb	skinless, boneless chicken breasts (about 4)	500 g
1/4 cup	all-purpose flour	50 mL
2 tsp	vegetable oil	10 mL

Sauce

1 cup	chicken stock	250 mL
3 tbsp	lemon juice	45 mL
2 tbsp	granulated sugar	25 mL
1 tbsp	vegetable oil	15 mL
4 tsp	cornstarch	20 mL
1 tsp	sesame oil	5 mL
1 tsp	grated lemon zest	5 mL
1/2 tsp	minced garlic	2 mL
2 tbsp	chopped fresh parsley	25 mL

1. In a large nonstick skillet sprayed with vegetable spray, heat 1 tsp (5 mL) oil over medium heat and sauté red peppers and peas just until tender-crisp (approximately 3 minutes). Place in a serving dish.

2. Between sheets of waxed paper, pound chicken breasts to 1/4-inch (5-mm) thickness. Dust with flour. In a large nonstick skillet sprayed with vegetable spray, heat oil; sauté chicken until browned on both sides and just cooked (for approximately 6 to 8 minutes).

3. In a saucepan combine stock, lemon juice, sugar, oil, cornstarch, sesame oil, lemon zest and garlic; cook over medium heat for 2 to 3 minutes or until thickened. Pour some sauce over chicken. Sprinkle with parsley. Serve individual servings with remaining sauce.

Black Bean, Corn and Leek Frittata

1 1/2 tsp	vegetable oil	7 mL
2 tsp	minced garlic	10 mL
3/4 cup	chopped leeks	175 mL
1/2 cup	chopped red bell peppers	125 mL
1/2 cup	canned or frozen corn kernels, drained	125 mL
1/2 cup	canned black beans, rinsed and drained	125 mL
1/3 cup	chopped fresh coriander	75 mL
2	eggs	2
3	egg whites	3
1/3 cup	2% milk	75 mL
1/4 tsp	salt	1 mL
1/4 tsp	freshly ground black pepper	1 mL
2 tbsp	grated Parmesan cheese	25 mL

1. In a nonstick saucepan sprayed with vegetable spray, heat oil over medium-high heat. Add garlic, leeks and red peppers; cook for 4 minutes or until softened. Remove from heat; stir in corn, black beans and coriander.

2. In a bowl whisk together whole eggs, egg whites, milk, salt and pepper. Stir in the cooled vegetable mixture.

3. Spray a 12-inch (30 cm) nonstick frying pan with vegetable spray. Heat over medium-low heat. Pour in the frittata mixture. Cook for 5 minutes, gently lifting the sides of the frittata to let uncooked egg mixture flow under the frittata. Sprinkle with Parmesan cheese. Cover and cook for another 3 minutes or until the frittata is set. Slip the frittata onto a serving platter.

4. Cut into wedges and serve immediately.

FROM
Rose Reisman's Light
Vegetarian Cooking

Chicken Breasts Stuffed with Brie Cheese, Red Pepper and Green Onions

Serves 4

TIP

Instead of serving each breast whole, slice each crosswise into medallions and fan out on plates.

•

Replace chicken with turkey, veal or pork scalopini.

•

Brie is a high-fat cheese, but 2 oz (50 g) divided among 4 servings makes it acceptable.

MAKE AHEAD

Prepare chicken breasts early in the day, sauté, then refrigerate. Bake for an extra 5 minutes just prior to serving.

PREHEAT OVEN TO 425° F (220° C)
BAKING SHEET SPRAYED WITH VEGETABLE SPRAY

2 oz	Brie cheese, at room temperature	50 g
3 tbsp	finely chopped red bell peppers	45 mL
3 tbsp	finely chopped green onions (about 2 medium)	45 mL
1 tsp	minced garlic	5 mL
1	egg	1
2 tbsp	2% milk	25 mL
1/2 cup	seasoned bread crumbs	125 mL
1 lb	skinless, boneless chicken breasts (about 4)	500 g
1 tbsp	vegetable oil	15 mL

1. In a small bowl, mix Brie cheese, red peppers, green onions and garlic. In another bowl whisk together egg and milk. Put bread crumbs on a plate.

2. Between sheets of waxed paper, pound breasts to 1/4-inch (5 mm) thickness. Put 1 tbsp (15 mL) Brie mixture at a short end of each breast. Roll up tightly; secure edge with a toothpick.

3. Dip each chicken roll in the egg wash, then in the bread crumbs. Heat oil in a large nonstick skillet sprayed with vegetable spray, cook over high heat for 3 minutes, turning often, or until browned on all sides. Put on prepared baking sheet and bake for 10 minutes or until just done at center. Remove toothpicks before serving.

FROM
Rose Reisman's Enlightened Home Cooking

Thick Rice Noodles with a Beef, Onion, Corn and Rosemary Sauce

Serves 4

Although this recipe works well with fettuccine, make an effort to find fresh thick rice noodles — they'll meld into the sauce and transform the everyday ingredients into a treasure of comfort food. Be generous with the hot sauce and slurp the noodles up with a fork and spoon.

1 lb	fresh rice noodles *or* fresh fettuccine	500 g
1 tsp	vegetable oil, plus oil for coating noodles	5 mL
8 oz	lean ground beef	250 g
1	onion, diced	1
1 tbsp	finely chopped rosemary	15 mL
1 cup	fresh or frozen corn kernels	250 mL
2 cups	beef or vegetable stock	500 mL
1 tbsp	cornstarch dissolved in 2 tbsp (25 mL) water	15 mL
	Salt and pepper to taste	
	Hot pepper sauce *or* sweet chili sauce	

1. If using fresh noodles, break them up by placing in a colander, running hot water over them and, if necessary, separating the strands with your fingers. (If using pasta, prepare according to package directions, drain and coat with a little oil.)

2. In a nonstick wok or skillet, heat oil over medium–high heat for 30 seconds. Add beef, onions and rosemary. Sauté, stirring often, until the beef is well browned. Drain the excess fat.

3. Add corn and stock and return to a boil. Add dissolved cornstarch and stir until the sauce begins to thicken. Season to taste with salt and pepper. Add noodles, mix well and heat until the noodles are soft, pliable and heated through, for about 2 or 3 minutes. (The dish will benefit from standing for a few minutes with the heat off; be careful not to leave it too long, however, or the noodles will become a starchy mass.) Serve with plenty of hot pepper sauce or sweet chili sauce.

FROM
New World Noodles
by Bill Jones and Stephen Wong

Makes 4 burgers

Mama's Italian Cheeseburgers

If burgers are starting to become mundane, put some excitement into those patties. Instead of cheese on top of the burger, put shredded cheese right in the ground meat mixture for moist burgers with a twist. Mama would be pleased.

TIP

For an easy vegetable topping, cut green or red bell peppers and a large red onion into rounds, brush lightly with olive oil and grill alongside burgers.

1/4 cup	tomato pasta sauce	50 mL
1/4 cup	grated or minced onion	50 mL
1	clove garlic, minced	1
1/4 tsp	dried basil *or* oregano	1 mL
1/4 tsp	salt	1 mL
1/4 tsp	pepper	1 mL
3/4 cup	shredded part-skim mozzarella *or* Fontina cheese	175 mL
1/3 cup	dry seasoned bread crumbs	75 mL
1 lb	lean ground beef	500 g
4	hamburger buns, split and lightly toasted	4

1. In a bowl combine tomato pasta sauce, onion, garlic, basil, salt and pepper. Stir in cheese and bread crumbs; mix in beef. Shape into four 3/4-inch (2 cm) thick patties.

2. Place on a greased grill over medium-high heat; cook, turning once, for 6 to 7 minutes on each side, or until no longer pink in the center. Serve in buns.

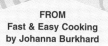

FROM
Fast & Easy Cooking
by Johanna Burkhard

Serves 4

We've somehow forgotten this delicious classic preparation — and it's worth considering again. Together, the golden red paprika and tangy sour cream bring out the best in tender veal and meaty mushrooms.

TIP

Fettuccine or broad egg noodles make a delicious companion to this creamy veal in mushroom sauce.

•

The most flavorful paprika comes from Hungary where it ranges in strength from mild (sweet) to hot.

FROM
The Comfort Food Cookbook
by Johanna Burkhard

Veal Paprikash

2 tbsp	vegetable oil	25 mL
1 lb	grain-fed veal scallops *or* boneless beef sirloin, cut into thin strips	500 g
4 cups	quartered mushrooms (about 12 oz [375 g])	1 L
1	large onion, halved lengthwise and thinly sliced	1
2	cloves garlic, minced	2
4 tsp	sweet Hungarian paprika	20 mL
1/2 tsp	dried marjoram	2 mL
1/2 tsp	salt	2 mL
1/4 tsp	pepper	1 mL
1 tbsp	all-purpose flour	15 mL
3/4 cup	chicken stock	175 mL
1/2 cup	sour cream	125 mL
	Salt and pepper	

1. In a large nonstick skillet, heat half of the oil over high heat; stir-fry veal in 2 batches, each for 3 minutes or until browned but still pink inside. Transfer to a plate along with pan juices; keep warm.

2.. Reduce heat to medium. Add remaining oil. Add mushrooms, onion, garlic, paprika, marjoram, salt and pepper; cook, stirring often, for 7 minutes or until lightly colored.

3. Sprinkle mushroom mixture with flour; pour in stock. Cook, stirring, for 2 minutes or until thickened. Stir in sour cream. Return veal and accumulated juices to pan; cook for 1 minute more or until heated through. Adjust seasoning with salt and pepper to taste; serve immediately.

Serves 4

TIP

Any small shell pasta can be used. Tri-color pasta gives lively appeal to this dish.

•

Select other favorite cheeses to substitute, such as Jarslberg, Romano or Havarti.

MAKE AHEAD

Prepare sauce early in the day. Reheat gently, adding more stock if too thick.

FROM
Rose Reisman Brings
Home Light Pasta

Four-Cheese Macaroni

8 oz	macaroni	250 g
1/4 cup	shredded Swiss cheese	50 mL
3 tbsp	shredded Cheddar cheese	45 mL
2 tbsp	grated Parmesan cheese	25 mL
1 1/2 oz	diced mozzarella cheese	40 g

Sauce

1 tbsp	margarine *or* butter	15 mL
2 tbsp	all-purpose flour	25 mL
1 cup	2% milk	250 mL
1 1/4 cups	chicken stock	300 mL
	Parsley	

1. Cook pasta in boiling water according to the package instructions or until firm to the bite. Drain and place in a serving bowl. Add Swiss, Cheddar, Parmesan and mozzarella cheeses.

2. Meanwhile, make the sauce: In a nonstick saucepan, melt margarine; add flour and cook for 1 minute, stirring constantly. Slowly add milk and chicken stock; stir constantly until sauce thickens, for approximately 4 minutes. Pour over pasta and toss well. Garnish with parsley.

Serves 4

Fresh salmon doesn't need much to enhance it, but this simple-to-prepare pesto sauce keeps the fish extra moist and adds a burst of fresh flavor.

TIP

Swordfish, tuna or halibut steaks can be substituted for salmon.

Double the quantity of the pesto ingredients; use half to marinate the fish and refrigerate the other half to use as a quick baste when grilling chicken, pork or lamb. Pesto can be refrigerated in a covered container for up to 1 week.

Simply Super Salmon with Lemon-Oregano Pesto

PREHEAT BARBECUE GRILL OR BROILER

1/2 cup	lightly packed parsley sprigs	125 mL
2 tbsp	chopped fresh oregano (or 2 tsp [10 mL] dried)	25 mL
1	clove garlic, minced	1
2 tbsp	olive oil	25 mL
2 tsp	grated lemon zest	10 mL
2 tbsp	freshly squeezed lemon juice	25 mL
	Salt and pepper	
1	salmon fillet, unskinned (about 1 1/4 lbs [625 g])	1

1. In a food processor or mini chopper, combine parsley, oregano, garlic, oil, lemon zest and lemon juice; season with salt and pepper to taste. Purée until very smooth.

2. Arrange salmon in a shallow glass dish; coat both sides with pesto. Let stand at room temperature for 15 minutes or cover and refrigerate for up to 2 hours.

3. Place the salmon skin-side down on greased grill over medium-high heat; cook for 4 to 5 minutes on each side (allow 10 minutes per 1-inch [2.5 cm] thickness) or until the fish is opaque and flakes easily with a fork. (Alternatively, arrange salmon on a broiler pan 4 inches [10 cm] below the broiler; cook for 5 minutes on each side or until the fish is opaque and flakes easily with a fork.) Cut the salmon into 4 portions and serve.

FROM
**Rose Reisman's Enlightened
Home Cooking**

Swordfish with Mango Coriander Salsa

Serves 6

TIP

Any firm fish can be substituted. Try tuna or shark.

•

Parsley or dill can be substituted for coriander. This salsa can be used over chicken or pork.

MAKE AHEAD

Make salsa early in the day and refrigerate.

START BARBECUE OR PREHEAT OVEN TO 425° F (220° C)

| 1 1/2 lbs | swordfish steaks | 750 g |
| 1 tsp | vegetable oil | 5 mL |

Salsa

1 1/2 cups	finely diced mango *or* peach	375 mL
3/4 cup	finely diced red peppers	175 mL
1/2 cup	finely diced green peppers	125 mL
1/2 cup	finely diced red onions	125 mL
1/4 cup	chopped fresh coriander	50 mL
2 tbsp	lemon juice	25 mL
2 tsp	olive oil	10 mL
1 tsp	minced garlic	5 mL

1. Brush the fish with 1 tsp (5 mL) of oil on both sides. Barbecue or bake fish for 10 minutes per 1-inch (2.5 cm) thickness, or until it flakes easily when pierced with a fork.

2. Meanwhile, in a bowl, combine mango, red peppers, green peppers, red onions, coriander, lemon juice, olive oil and garlic; mix thoroughly. Serve over the fish.

Salmon over White-and Black-Bean Salsa

TIP

Swordfish or tuna can be substituted for salmon.

•

Other varieties of beans can be substituted if black or white navy beans are unavailable.

•

If you're not using canned beans, 1 cup (250 mL) dry yields 3 cups (750 mL) cooked.

START BARBECUE OR PREHEAT OVEN TO 425° F (220° C)

Salsa

1 cup	canned black beans, drained	250 mL
1 cup	canned white navy beans, drained	250 mL
3/4 cup	chopped tomatoes	175 mL
1/2 cup	chopped green peppers	125 mL
1/4 cup	chopped red onions	50 mL
1/4 cup	chopped fresh coriander	50 mL
2 tbsp	balsamic vinegar	25 mL
2 tbsp	lemon juice	25 mL
1 tbsp	olive oil	15 mL
1 tsp	minced garlic	5 mL
1 lb	salmon steaks	500 g

1. Salsa: In a bowl combine black beans, white beans, tomatoes, green peppers, red onions and coriander. In a small bowl, whisk together vinegar, lemon juice, olive oil and garlic; pour over bean mixture and toss to combine.

2. Barbecue the fish or bake uncovered for approximately 10 minutes for each 1-inch (2.5 cm) thickness of fish, or until the fish flakes with a fork. Serve fish over bean salsa.

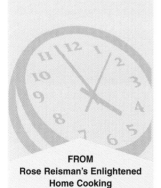

FROM
Rose Reisman's Enlightened Home Cooking

Linguine with Caramelized Onions, Tomatoes and Basil

Serves 4

TIP

Try Vidalia onions when in season (usually in the spring).

•

If using fresh basil, you'll get a more pronounced flavor if you add the basil after the pasta is tossed with the sauce. (Dried basil is added during the cooking.)

MAKE AHEAD

Cook onions 1 day in advance. Reheat, then continue recipe.

2 tsp	vegetable oil	10 mL
2 tsp	minced garlic	10 mL
2 tbsp	packed brown sugar	25 mL
6 cups	thinly sliced red onions	1.5 L
2 cups	diced plum tomatoes	500 mL
3/4 cup	vegetable stock	175 mL
1/2 cup	chopped fresh basil (or 1 1/2 tsp [7 mL] dried)	125 mL
1/4 tsp	freshly ground black pepper	1 mL
12 oz	linguine	375 g

1. In a large nonstick saucepan, heat oil over medium-low heat. Add garlic, sugar and red onions; cook, stirring often, for 30 minutes or until browned and very soft.

2. Stir in tomatoes, stock, basil and pepper; cook for 5 minutes longer or until heated through.

3. Meanwhile, in a pot of boiling water, cook linguine until tender but firm. Drain and toss with sauce.

FROM
Rose Reisman's
Light Vegetarian Cooking

Serves 6

TIP

For a sharper flavor, try using Romano cheese as a replacement for Parmesan.

•

Broccoli can replace asparagus.

MAKE AHEAD

Prepare sauce early in day. Reheat gently, adding more stock if sauce thickens.

FROM
Rose Reisman Brings
Home Light Pasta

Rotini Alfredo with Asparagus, Sweet Red Pepper and Prosciutto

12 oz	rotini	375 g
2 cups	chopped asparagus	500 mL
1 1/4 cups	thinly sliced sweet red peppers	300 mL
1/3 cup	chopped prosciutto *or* smoked ham	75 mL

Sauce

1 tbsp	margarine *or* butter	15 mL
2 tbsp	all-purpose flour	25 mL
1 1/4 cup	2% milk	300 mL
1 cup	chicken or beef stock	250 mL
1/3 cup	grated Parmesan cheese	75 mL
Pinch	nutmeg	Pinch
Pinch	black pepper	Pinch

1. Cook pasta in boiling water according to the package instructions or until firm to the bite. Drain and place in a serving bowl.

2. Cook asparagus in boiling water just until tender, for approximately 3 minutes. Drain and rinse with cold water. Add to pasta. Cook red peppers in boiling water for 1 minute. Drain and rinse with cold water, and add to pasta. Add prosciutto.

3. Make the sauce: In a small nonstick skillet, melt margarine; add flour and cook for 1 minute, stirring constantly. Add milk and stock; simmer on medium heat, stirring constantly until slightly thickened, for approximately 4 minutes. Add cheese, nutmeg and pepper. Pour over pasta, and toss.

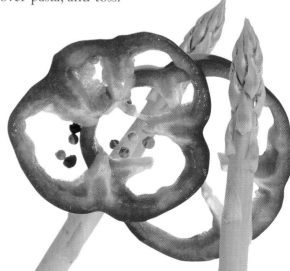

Vegetables
and Side Dishes

Serves 4

Rapini with Balsamic Vinegar

Some of the healthiest vegetables are also the least popular — particularly bitter greens like dandelions and rapini. Why? Mostly because they are so often treated like spinach, steamed slightly and served either plain or buttered as a side vegetable. Done that way they taste like poison.

•

To see how bitter greens can be made delicious we must look to the Italians, who use their unrivaled condiments and cheeses to create just the kind of culinary sorcery needed to make the greens pleasurable. These enhancements — which include olive oil, balsamic vinegar and Parmesan cheese — lend flavors and qualities that work with the bitterness and make it interesting.

•

This salad can be served immediately, or it can wait, covered and unrefrigerated for up to 1 hour.

1	bunch rapini, washed, bottom 1 1/2 inches (3 cm) of stalks trimmed	1
1 tsp	salt	5 mL
3 tbsp	balsamic vinegar	45 mL
2 tbsp	extra virgin olive oil	25 mL
	black pepper to taste	
	few sprigs fresh basil *or* parsley, chopped	
1/4 cup	thinly sliced red onions	50 mL
1 tsp	drained capers	5 mL
3 tbsp	shaved Parmesan *or* Pecorino cheese	45 mL

1. Cut off the top 2 1/2 inches (6 cm) of rapini — the part that has the leaves and the flowers — and set aside. Cut the remaining stalks into 1-inch (2.5 cm) pieces.

2. In a large pot, bring 1 1/2 inches (3 cm) of water to a boil. Add the salt and chopped stalks and cook uncovered for 8 minutes, until tender. Add the reserved tops and cook for another 8 minutes, uncovered. Drain, refresh with cold water, and drain again.

3. Transfer the drained rapini to a serving plate and spread out. In a small bowl, combine vinegar, olive oil, pepper to taste and chopped basil or parsley. Evenly dress the rapini with this sauce. Scatter slices of red onion and capers over the rapini, and top with shaved cheese.

FROM
The New Vegetarian Gourmet
by Byron Ayanoglu

Lemon-Glazed Baby Carrots

Serves 4

This is one of my favorite choices to accompany a holiday roast or turkey. Packages of ready-to-cook, peeled whole baby carrots are widely available in supermarkets. They certainly make a cook's life easier — especially when you're preparing a mammoth family dinner and plan to serve several dishes.

TIP

If doubling the recipe, glaze vegetables in a large nonstick skillet to evaporate the stock quickly.

•

Try this tasty treatment with a combination of blanched carrots, rutabaga and parsnip strips, too.

1 lb	peeled baby carrots	500 g
1/4 cup	chicken stock *or* vegetable stock	50 mL
1 tbsp	butter	15 mL
1 tbsp	brown sugar	15 mL
1 tbsp	lemon juice	15 mL
1/2 tsp	grated lemon rind	2 mL
1/4 tsp	salt	1 mL
	Pepper to taste	
1 tbsp	finely chopped fresh parsley *or* chives	15 mL

1. In a medium saucepan, cook the carrots in boiling salted water for 5 to 7 minutes (start timing when water returns to a boil) or until just tender-crisp; drain and return to the saucepan.

2. Add stock, butter, brown sugar, lemon juice and rind, salt and pepper. Cook, stirring often, for 3 to 5 minutes or until the liquid has evaporated and the carrots are nicely glazed.

3. Sprinkle with parsley or chives and serve.

FROM
The Comfort Food Cookbook
by Johanna Burkhard

Serves 4

TIP

Use ricotta cheese instead of cottage cheese for a creamier consistency. There will, however, be slightly more calories per serving.

MAKE AHEAD

Prepare and refrigerate up to a day before. Bake just before serving.

Cheese and Red Pepper Stuffed Potatoes

PREHEAT OVEN TO 425° F (220° C)

2	large baking potatoes	2
1/3 cup	2% cottage cheese	75 mL
1/4 cup	2% yogurt	50 mL
2 tbsp	2% milk	25 mL
1 tsp	vegetable oil	5 mL
1 1/2 tsp	crushed garlic	7 mL
1/4 cup	finely diced onion	50 mL
1/4 cup	finely diced red bell pepper	50 mL
2 tbsp	chopped fresh dill (or 1 tsp [5 mL] dried)	25 mL
	Salt and pepper	
2 tbsp	grated Parmesan cheese	25 mL

1. Pierce potatoes with a fork; bake or microwave just until tender. Cool and slice lengthwise in half; carefully scoop out the pulp, leaving shell intact. Place pulp in a mixing bowl or food processor.

2. Add cottage cheese, yogurt and milk; mix well. (Or process using on/off motion; do not purée.) Set aside.

3. In a nonstick skillet, heat oil; sauté garlic, onion and red pepper until tender. Add dill, and salt and pepper to taste; add to potato mixture and mix well. Do not purée.

4. Stuff into potato shells; sprinkle with Parmesan cheese. Place on a baking sheet and bake for 10 minutes or until hot.

FROM
Rose Reisman Brings
Home Light Cooking

Serves 4

Spicy Rice with Feta Cheese and Black Olives

1 tbsp	vegetable oil	15 mL
2 tsp	crushed garlic	10 mL
1/2 cup	chopped onion	125 mL
1/2 cup	chopped zucchini	125 mL
1/4 cup	chopped red bell pepper	50 mL
1 cup	rice	250 mL
1 1/2 cups	chicken stock	375 mL
1 tsp	dried oregano	5 mL
1 tsp	dried basil	5 mL
1 tsp	chili powder	5 mL
1/4 cup	sliced pitted black olives	50 mL
2 oz	feta cheese, crumbled	50 g

1. In a large nonstick saucepan, heat oil; sauté garlic, onion, zucchini and red pepper until softened, for approximately 5 minutes. Add rice and brown for 2 minutes, stirring constantly.

2. Add stock, oregano, basil, chili powder and olives; cover and simmer for approximately 20 minutes or until the rice is tender. Pour into a serving dish and sprinkle with cheese.

FROM
Rose Reisman Brings
Home Light Cooking

Piedmont Peppers

Within this simple preparation resides the essence of rustic Italian cooking: startlingly fresh ingredients, simply paired and quickly put together. It has color, an easy style, incredible flavor and a wonderful history. If you make no other recipe from this book make this one — you will be astonished at just how good it is. Include lots of earthy, rustic country-style bread alongside to mop up the juices.

Don't choose overly huge peppers for this dish. While yellow or orange peppers can be used, green peppers just don't have the requisite depth of flavor.

•

In Piedmont they seem to have a penchant for stuffing. Besides peppers, they stuff onions with a sweet and savory filling that includes raisins, cheese and eggs. Mushrooms are filled with their own chopped stems combined with parsley, onions, anchovies and bread crumbs. Perhaps best of all, fresh peach halves are treated to a heavenly filling of crushed macaroons blended with egg, butter and sugar before being baked.

FROM
Rustic Italian Cooking
by Kathleen Sloan

PREHEAT OVEN TO 350° F (180° C)
13- BY 9-INCH (3 L) BAKING DISH, OILED

6	red bell peppers, halved and seeded, stems left intact	6
6	plum tomatoes, peeled and quartered	6
12	anchovy fillets, rinsed and roughly chopped	6
4	cloves garlic, thinly sliced	4
1/2 cup	extra virgin olive oil	125 mL
	Salt and freshly ground black pepper	
12	whole leaves flat-leaf parsley	12

1. Lay peppers in the prepared baking dish, cut-side up, in one layer. Into each pepper cavity, place two pieces of tomato. Sprinkle with chopped anchovies, making sure each pepper gets the equivalent of a whole anchovy fillet. Evenly distribute the sliced garlic among the peppers. Carefully pour the olive oil over the peppers. Sprinkle with just a little bit of salt (because of anchovies) and lots of freshly ground black pepper.

2. Roast in the top half of preheated oven for 1 hour or until the peppers are tender. Cool slightly. Serve warm, garnished with parsley leaves.

Jalapeno Broccoli

Serves 4 to 5

The stubby, lush green chilies that take their name from the Mexican city of Jalapa (in the state of Vera Cruz) have become as common in our markets as they are in their home country. Here is a recipe that uses their sweet heat to dress up therapeutic broccoli and actually makes it fun to eat.

•

This salad can be served immediately or it can wait up to 2 hours, covered and unrefrigerated.

1 tsp	salt	5 mL
1	head broccoli, trimmed and separated into spears	1
1 tbsp	balsamic vinegar	15 mL
2–3 tbsp	olive oil	25–45 mL
2	fresh jalapeno peppers, thinly sliced (with or without seeds, depending on desired hotness)	2
1/4 cup	toasted pine nuts	50 mL
	Few sprigs fresh coriander *or* parsley, chopped	

1. Bring a pot of water to boil and add salt. Add the broccoli spears and boil over high heat for 3 to 5 minutes (depending on desired tenderness). Drain and transfer broccoli to a bowl of ice cold water for 30 seconds. Drain and lay out the cooked spears decoratively on a presentation plate. Drizzle evenly with balsamic vinegar.

2. In a small frying pan, heat olive oil over medium heat for 30 seconds. Add sliced jalapeno peppers (with seeds, if using) and stir-fry for 2 to 3 minutes until softened. Take peppers with all the oil from the pan, and distribute evenly over the broccoli. Garnish with pine nuts and herbs.

FROM
The New Vegetarian Gourmet
by Byron Ayanoglu

Serves 4

TIP

Add a sprinkle of fresh herbs such as parsley or basil to the oil mixture.

MAKE AHEAD

These peppers can be prepared ahead of time and served cold.

FROM
Rose Reisman Brings
Home Light Cooking

Roasted Garlic Sweet Pepper Strips

PREHEAT OVEN TO 400° F (200° C)

4	large sweet peppers (combination of green, red and yellow)	4
2 tbsp	olive oil	25 mL
1 1/2 tsp	crushed garlic	7 mL
1 tbsp	grated Parmesan cheese	15 mL

1. On a baking sheet, bake whole peppers for 15 to 20 minutes, turning occasionally, or until blistered and blackened. Place in paper bag; seal and let stand for 10 minutes.

2. Peel off charred skin from the peppers; cut off tops and bottoms. Remove seeds and ribs; cut into 1-inch (2.5 cm) wide strips and place on serving platter.

3. Mix oil with garlic; brush over peppers. Sprinkle with cheese.

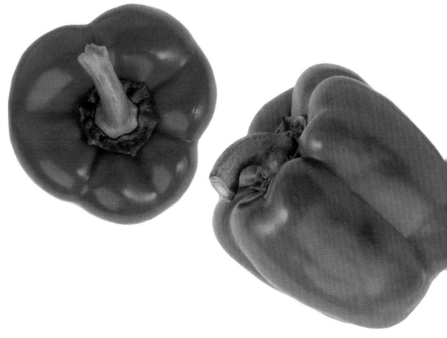

Serves 4

The simple addition of cashews and red onions to this dish transforms ordinary green beans into a formidable companion to any gourmet main course.

Green Beans with Cashews

1 lb	green beans, trimmed	500 g
2 tbsp	olive oil	25 mL
1/2 cup	slivered red onions	125 mL
1/3 cup	raw cashews	75 mL
1/4 tsp	salt	1 mL
1/4 tsp	black pepper	1 mL
	Few sprigs fresh parsley, chopped	

1. Blanch green beans in a pot of boiling water for 5 minutes. Drain and immediately refresh in a bowl of ice-cold water. Drain and set aside.

2. In a large frying pan heat olive oil over medium-high heat for 30 seconds. Add onions, cashews, salt and pepper and stir-fry for 2 to 3 minutes, until the onions are softened. Add cooked green beans, raise heat to high, and stir-fry actively for 2 to 3 minutes, until the beans feel hot to the touch. (Take care that you don't burn any cashews in the process.) Transfer to a serving plate and garnish with chopped parsley. Serve immediately.

FROM
The New Vegetarian Gourmet
by Byron Ayanoglu

FROM
**Rose Reisman's Enlightened
Home Cooking**

Asparagus, Red Pepper and Goat Cheese Phyllo Roll

Serves 8

TIP

If goat cheese is not available, use grated mozzarella or Cheddar cheese.

•

Substitute thinly sliced ham (preferably smoked) for prosciutto.

•

When cutting this magnificent-looking vegetable dish, be sure to use a sharp knife.

MAKE AHEAD

Cook asparagus and rinse with cold water. Prepare cheese filling and cook vegetables before baking.

PREHEAT OVEN TO 375° F (190° C)
BAKING SHEET SPRAYED WITH VEGETABLE SPRAY

6 oz	asparagus spears, trimmed	175 g
Filling		
1 tsp	oil	5 mL
1 1/2 tsp	minced garlic	7 mL
1 1/2 cups	chopped red bell peppers	375 mL
1/4 cup	chopped green onions	50 mL
1/3 cup	5% ricotta cheese	75 mL
3 oz	goat cheese	75 g
1	egg	1
2 tbsp	grated Parmesan cheese	25 mL
1/4 tsp	coarsely grated pepper	1 mL
5	sheets phyllo pastry	5
2 tsp	margarine *or* butter, melted	10 mL
1 oz	sliced prosciutto	25 g

1. In a saucepan of boiling water or in the microwave, cook asparagus for 3 minutes or until tender; drain and set aside.

2. In a nonstick skillet over medium heat, add oil and cook garlic and red peppers for 5 minutes or until tender; add green onions and cook for 1 minute more. Remove from heat.

3. In a bowl, combine ricotta and goat cheeses, egg, Parmesan and pepper; mix until smooth.

4. Keeping remaining phyllo covered with a cloth to prevent drying out, layer two sheets of phyllo one on top of the other; brush with melted margarine. Layer two more sheets of phyllo on top; brush with melted margarine. Put last phyllo sheet on top. Spread cheese mixture evenly over top. Spread the prosciutto slices along one of the long sides, top it with the sweet pepper mixture, and put the asparagus spears on top. Starting from the long edge where the filling is, roll the phyllo and filling jelly roll fashion. Tuck the ends under and place on prepared baking sheet. Brush with remaining melted margarine and bake for 20 to 25 minutes, or until golden brown. Cut into slices and serve.

TIP

If desired, use 8 jumbo mushrooms, but add 1/4 cup (50 mL) water to baking pan so they do not dry out.

•

Goat cheese can replace feta.

MAKE AHEAD

Stuff mushrooms up to a day ahead. Keep refrigerated. Bake just before serving.

Mushrooms with Creamy Feta Cheese and Dill Stuffing

PREHEAT OVEN TO 425° F (220° C)

16	medium mushrooms	16
1 tsp	vegetable oil	5 mL
1 1/2 tsp	minced garlic	7 mL
1/3 cup	finely chopped onions	75 mL
1/3 cup	finely chopped red or green bell peppers	75 mL
1/3 cup	crumbled feta cheese	75 mL
3 tbsp	5% ricotta cheese	45 mL
2 tbsp	chopped fresh dill (or 1 tsp [5 mL] dried)	25 mL
2 tbsp	finely chopped green onions (about 1 medium)	25 mL

1. Remove the stems from the mushrooms; set caps aside and dice stems.

2. In a small nonstick saucepan sprayed with vegetable spray, heat oil over medium heat; add diced mushroom stems, garlic, onions and peppers. Cook for 5 minutes, or until softened. Remove from heat.

3. Add feta cheese, ricotta cheese, dill and green onions; mix well. Carefully stuff the mixture into the mushroom caps. Place in a baking dish and bake for 15 to 20 minutes or just until the mushrooms release their liquid.

FROM
Rose Reisman's Enlightened Home Cooking

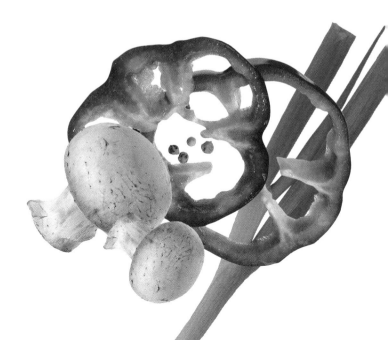

FROM
Rose Reisman's
Light Vegetarian Cooking

Sugar Snap Peas with Sesame Sauce

Serves 4

TIP

Use snow peas or green beans instead of the sugar snap peas.

MAKE AHEAD

Prepare sauce up to 2 days in advance.

•

Best cooked right before serving.

1 tbsp	honey	15 mL
1 tbsp	rice wine vinegar	15 mL
1 tbsp	sesame oil	15 mL
1 tbsp	soya sauce	15 mL
1/2 tsp	minced garlic	2 mL
1 lb	sugar snap peas, trimmed	500 g
1 tsp	vegetable oil	5 mL
1 tbsp	toasted sesame seeds	15 mL

1. In a small bowl, combine honey, vinegar, sesame oil, soya sauce and garlic; set aside.

2. Steam or boil sugar peas for 2 minutes. In a large non-stick skillet sprayed with vegetable spray, heat oil over medium-high heat; cook peas for 3 minutes or until tender-crisp. Pour sauce over peas; cook until heated through. Serve immediately, sprinkled with sesame seeds.

Serves 4 to 6

Eggplant with Goat Cheese and Roasted Sweet Peppers

TIP

Feta cheese, grated Cheddar or Swiss can replace goat cheese. A stronger tasting cheese suits this dish.

•

Either use bottled-in-water roasted red peppers or, under a broiler, roast a small pepper for 15 to 20 minutes or until charred. Cool, then peel, deseed and chop. Use remainder for another purpose.

MAKE AHEAD

Prepare the entire dish early in the day. Bake just before serving.

PREHEAT OVEN TO 350° F (180° C)
BAKING SHEET SPRAYED WITH VEGETABLE SPRAY

1	egg	1
1/4 cup	2% milk	50 mL
3/4 cup	seasoned bread crumbs	175 mL
2 tbsp	vegetable oil	25 mL
10	1/2-inch (1 cm) slices eggplant, skin on	10
3 oz	goat cheese	75 g
3 tbsp	2% milk	45 mL
3 tbsp	chopped roasted red peppers	45 mL
1/4 cup	chopped green onions (about 2 medium)	50 mL
1/2 tsp	minced garlic	2 mL

1. Beat egg and milk together in a small bowl. Put the bread crumbs on a plate. Dip the eggplant slices in the egg wash then press into bread crumbs. In a large non-stick skillet sprayed with vegetable spray, heat 1 tbsp (15 mL) of the oil over medium heat. Add half of the breaded eggplant slices and cook for 4 minutes or until golden brown on both sides. Add the remaining 1 tbsp (15 mL) oil and respray the skillet with vegetable spray. Repeat with the remaining eggplant slices. Place on prepared baking sheet.

2. In a small bowl, stir together goat cheese, milk, red peppers, green onions and garlic. Put a spoonful of topping on top of each eggplant slice. Bake for 10 minutes or until heated through.

FROM
Rose Reisman's Enlightened
Home Cooking

Cheese and Salsa Quesadillas

Serves 4

Here's my modern rendition of grilled cheese: thin flour tortillas replace sliced bread, mozzarella substitutes for processed cheese and chunky salsa stands in for the ketchup. And the beans? They're optional, but make a wholesome addition.

TIP

I often serve these warm cheesy wedges with soup for an easy dinner. They're also great as a snack that both kids and grownups applaud.

•

Use mild salsa to appease those with timid taste buds, but add a dash of hot pepper sauce to the filling for those who like a burst of heat.

1/2 cup	prepared salsa, plus additional for serving	125 mL
4	flour tortillas (8-inch [20 cm] size)	4
1 cup	canned black or pinto beans, rinsed and drained well	250 mL
1 cup	shredded mozzarella, Monterey Jack or Cheddar cheese	250 mL

1. Spread 2 tbsp (25 mL) salsa on one-half of each tortilla. Sprinkle with 1/4 cup (50 mL) each of the beans and the cheese. Fold tortillas over and press down lightly.

2. Heat a large nonstick skillet over medium heat; cook tortillas, 2 at a time, pressing down lightly with the back of a metal spatula, for about 2 minutes per side, until lightly toasted and the cheese is melted. Or, place directly on the barbecue grill over medium heat until lightly toasted on both sides.

3. Cut into wedges and serve warm with additional salsa, if desired.

FROM
The Comfort Food Cookbook
by Johanna Burkhard

When the palate demands the wonderful taste of fried potatoes, but the waistline says "no" to French fries, try this zesty re-fry of par-boiled potato. It uses a minimum of oil, and delivers delightful flavors.

Herbed Potatoes

1 lb	new potatoes (about 3), unpeeled but well scrubbed	500 g
1/4 cup	olive oil	50 mL
1/4 tsp	salt	1 mL
1/4 tsp	black pepper	1 mL
1 tbsp	lemon zest	15 mL
4	cloves garlic, finely chopped	4
	Few sprigs fresh parsley and/or rosemary, chopped	
2 tbsp	lemon juice	25 mL

1. In a large saucepan, boil the potatoes over high heat for 5 to 7 minutes, until they can just be pierced with a fork. Drain and refresh several times with cold water. Cut the potatoes into 1/2-inch (1 cm) rounds.

2. In a large frying pan heat oil over high heat for 30 seconds. Add salt and pepper and stir. Add potatoes in a single layer and fry for 2 to 3 minutes; reduce the heat to medium-high, turn rounds over and fry the other side for 2 to 3 minutes, then toss-fry for another 1 to 2 minutes until golden all over. (Some of the skins will have peeled off and fried to a crisp; don't worry, they'll add to the final appeal.)

3. Add lemon zest, garlic and most of the chopped herb(s), reserving some for the final garnish. Toss-fry for 1 to 2 minutes. Add the lemon juice and toss-fry for 1 to 2 minutes until the sizzle has stopped and the acidity of the lemon has mellowed. (Taste a piece.) Transfer the potatoes to a serving bowl and garnish with the remainder of the herb(s). Serve immediately.

FROM
The New Vegetarian Gourmet
by Byron Ayanoglu

Desserts

Serves 6 to 8

Intimidated by the thought of making two-crust pies? Try this simple free-form pie – it only needs a single pie crust and looks like it came from a pastry shop.

TIP

Store-bought pastry for a single crust pie can be used instead of the suggested homemade pastry.

Farmhouse Apple Pie

PREHEAT OVEN TO 375° F (190° C)
LARGE BAKING SHEET, LIGHTLY GREASED

Pastry

1 1/4 cups	all-purpose flour	300 mL
1 tbsp	granulated sugar	15 mL
Pinch	salt	Pinch
1/2 cup	butter, cut into pieces	125 mL
2 tbsp	cold water (approximate)	25 mL

Filling

4	apples, such as Golden Delicious, Spy or Granny Smith, peeled, cored and sliced	4
1/3 cup	granulated sugar	75 mL
1/4 cup	finely chopped pecans	50 mL
1/2 tsp	cinnamon	2 mL

1. Pastry: In a bowl, combine flour, sugar and a generous pinch of salt. Cut in butter with a pastry blender or use your fingertips to make coarse crumbs. Sprinkle with enough water to hold the dough together; gather into a ball. Flatten to a 5-inch (12 cm) circle; wrap in plastic wrap and refrigerate for 30 minutes.

2. On a lightly floured board, roll pastry to a 13-inch (32 cm) circle; transfer to the baking sheet. Using a sharp knife, trim the pastry edge to form an even circle.

3. Filling: Starting 2 inches (5 cm) from the edge, overlap apple slices in a circle; arrange another overlapping circle of apples in the center. In a bowl, combine sugar, pecans and cinnamon; sprinkle over the apples. Fold pastry rim over apples to form a 2-inch (5 cm) edge.

4. Bake for 35 to 40 minutes or until the pastry is golden and the apples are tender. Place on a rack to let cool. With a spatula, carefully slide pie onto a serving platter.

FROM
Fast & Easy Cooking
by Johanna Burkhard

Makes 16 squares

Lemon Poppy Seed Squares

TIP

Here's an updated version of the comfort food classic, lemon squares — but with much less fat and calories.

•

Try substituting lime juice and zest for the lemon.

MAKE AHEAD

Prepare up to 2 days in advance.

PREHEAT OVEN TO 350° F (180° C)
8-INCH SQUARE (2 L) BAKING PAN SPRAYED WITH
VEGETABLE SPRAY

Cake

1/2 cup	granulated sugar	125 mL
1 tbsp	margarine *or* butter	15 mL
2 tsp	poppy seeds	10 mL
1 1/2 tsp	grated lemon zest	7 mL
1	egg	1
3/4 cup	cake and pastry flour	175 mL

Topping

2/3 cup	granulated sugar	150 mL
2 tsp	grated lemon zest	10 mL
1/3 cup	freshly squeezed lemon juice	75 mL
1 tbsp	cornstarch	15 mL
1	egg	1
1	egg white	1

1. Make the cake: In a bowl whisk together sugar, margarine, poppy seeds, lemon zest and egg until smooth. Add wet ingredients to flour and stir until mixed. Pat into the prepared pan; set aside.

2. Make the topping: In a bowl stir together sugar, lemon zest, lemon juice, cornstarch, whole egg and egg white. Pour over cake batter in the pan.

3. Bake 20 to 25 minutes or until set with the center still slightly soft. Cool to room temperature on a wire rack.

FROM
Rose Reisman's
Light Vegetarian Cooking

Makes 12 muffins

Blueberry Banana Muffins

TIP

A 9- by 5-inch (2 L) loaf pan can also be used; bake for 30 to 40 minutes or until tester comes out dry.

•

Use the ripest bananas possible for the best flavor.

MAKE AHEAD

Bake a day before or freeze for up to 6 weeks.

PREHEAT OVEN TO 375° F (190° C)
12 MUFFIN CUPS SPRAYED WITH VEGETABLE SPRAY

3/4 cup	puréed bananas (about 1 1/2 bananas)	175 mL
1/2 cup	granulated sugar	125 mL
1/3 cup	vegetable oil	75 mL
1	egg	1
1 tsp	vanilla	5 mL
1 cup	all–purpose flour	250 mL
1 tsp	baking powder	5 mL
1 tsp	baking soda	5 mL
1/4 cup	2% yogurt *or* light sour cream	50 mL
1/2 cup	blueberries	125 mL

1. In a large bowl, beat together bananas, sugar, oil, egg and vanilla until well mixed.

2. Combine flour, baking powder and baking soda; stir into a bowl. Stir in yogurt and fold in blueberries.

3. Pour batter into the prepared muffin cups; bake for approximately 20 minutes or until tops are firm to the touch.

FROM
Rose Reisman Brings
Home Light Cooking

Lemon Fool with Fresh Berries

Here's an updated version of the traditional "fool" — an old-fashioned dessert with fruit or berries folded into whipped cream or custard. This dessert is ideal for entertaining since it can be assembled earlier in the day.

TIP

Instead of individual serving dishes, layer berries and lemon fool in a 6-cup (1.5 L) deep glass serving bowl.

2 tbsp	cornstarch	25 mL
2/3 cup	granulated sugar	150 mL
1 tbsp	grated lemon zest	15 mL
1/3 cup	freshly squeezed lemon juice	75 mL
2	egg yolks	2
1 cup	whipping (35%) cream	250 mL
3 cups	fresh berries, such as sliced strawberries or raspberries or blueberries	750 mL
	Additional berries, mint sprigs and grated lemon zest	

1. In a small saucepan, combine cornstarch with 1/2 cup (125 mL) cold water; whisk until smooth. Add sugar, lemon zest, juice and egg yolks; cook over medium heat, whisking constantly, until the mixture comes to a full boil; cook for 15 seconds. Remove from heat; pour into a large bowl. Let cool slightly. Cover surface with plastic wrap; refrigerate for 2 hours or until chilled. (Recipe can be prepared to this point up to a day ahead.)

2. In a bowl using an electric mixer, whip cream until still peaks form. Whisk lemon mixture until smooth. Whisk in one-quarter of the whipped cream; fold in remaining whipped cream.

3. Arrange half the berries in 6 parfait or large wine glasses. Top with half the lemon fool; layer with remaining berries and lemon fool. (Recipe can be prepared to this point and refrigerated for up to 4 hours.) To serve, garnish with whole berries, mint sprigs and grated lemon zest.

FROM
Fast & Easy Cooking
by Johanna Burkhard

As close to heaven as a sexy dessert can get. If you don't have a double boiler in which to make the sauce (or a zabaglione, as this particular one is referred to in Italy), improvise with one small saucepan set inside a larger one filled with hot (not boiling) water.

If you can find them, try this beautiful dish with ripe black figs split in half; no need to cook them beforehand.

Use the best fruits of the season: strawberries in spring, figs in late summer and pears in autumn and winter.

**FROM
Rustic Italian Cooking
by Kathleen Sloan**

Baked Pears

PREHEAT BROILER
BRUSH A FLAT CERAMIC OR GLASS BAKING DISH WITH OIL

1 tsp	almond oil *or* walnut oil *or* any light tasting oil	5 mL
12	small ripe pears, peeled, trimmed, seeded and quartered	12
4	egg yolks	4
1/4 cup	Marsala *or* dry sherry	50 mL
1/4 cup	sugar	50 mL

1. Lay poached pears in prepared dish.

2. In a double boiler, or mixing bowl over a saucepan of hot (not boiling) water, whisk together egg yolks, Marsala and sugar for about 7 to 10 minutes or until doubled in volume, foamy and light.

3. Pour zabaglione over the pears and place under the broiler, for 1 to 2 minutes, or just until the top begins to brown in patches. (Be sure to watch it carefully.) Serve immediately.

Chocolate Fondue

Serves 2

This one is for lovers. The two of you can invoke St. Valentine any day of the year with a pot of melted chocolate, some fruit, biscuits and a lot of affection.

4 oz	fine chocolate, preferably bittersweet, broken into pieces	125 g
2 tbsp	Frangelico liqueur	25 mL
1 tbsp	water	15 mL
	Assorted imported biscuits (wafers, piroulines, petits-beurres, shortbreads)	
	Assorted fruit slices (plum, peach, banana, mango, starfruit)	

1. Melt the chocolate with Frangelico and water in the top of a double boiler set over (not in) hot water, for about 10 minutes.

2. Meanwhile, take your prettiest serving platter and decorate the edges with biscuits and fruits and 2 dainty forks. Leave a space in the middle for the chocolate.

3. Test the chocolate mixture by poking it with a fork: if it goes right through with no resistance, the chocolate is ready; if not, continue cooking for up to 5 minutes more. When the chocolate is extremely soft (miraculously, it still retains its shape), remove the double boiler from the heat. Using a fork or a small whisk, beat the chocolate for 1 to 2 minutes until all the liquids have been incorporated.

4. Transfer the chocolate to a beautiful bowl (crystal is best) and position at the center of your serving platter. Now you and your mate are free to cuddle up and dip fruit and biscuits into the chocolate.

FROM
The New Vegetarian Gourmet
by Byron Ayanoglu

Mocha Brownies with Cream Cheese Icing

PREHEAT OVEN TO 350° F (180° C)
8-INCH (2 L) SQUARE CAKE PAN SPRAYED WITH
VEGETABLE SPRAY

1/3 cup	margarine *or* butter	75 mL
3/4 cup	granulated sugar	175 mL
1	egg	1
2 tsp	instant coffee granules	10 mL
1 tbsp	warm water	15 mL
1/3 cup	unsweetened cocoa	75 mL
1/3 cup	all-purpose flour	75 mL
1 tsp	baking powder	5 mL
1/4 cup	2% yogurt	50 mL

Icing

1/4 cup	light cream cheese, softened	50 mL
1/2 cup	icing sugar	125 mL

1. In a bowl, cream together margarine and sugar until smooth. Add egg and mix well. Dissolve coffee granules in the warm water; add to batter and beat until well combined. (Mixture may look curdled.)

2. In a small bowl, stir together cocoa, flour and baking powder; add to the batter alternately with yogurt, stirring just until blended. Pour batter into the prepared pan and bake for 20 minutes, or until edges begin to pull away from the pan (center will be still slightly soft). Let cool.

3. Icing: In a small bowl, beat together cream cheese and icing sugar until smooth. Spread over top of the brownies.

Cream Cheese-Filled Brownies

Makes 12 to 16 squares

MAKE AHEAD

Prepare up to 2 days in advance. Freeze up to 4 weeks.

PREHEAT OVEN TO 350° F (180° C)
8-INCH (2 L) SQUARE BAKING DISH SPRAYED WITH
VEGETABLE SPRAY

Filling

4 oz	light cream cheese, softened	125 g
2 tbsp	granulated sugar	25 mL
2 tbsp	2% milk	25 mL
1 tsp	vanilla extract	5 mL

Cake

1 cup	packed brown sugar	250 mL
1/3 cup	light sour cream	75 mL
1/4 cup	vegetable oil	50 mL
1	egg	1
1	egg white	1
3/4 cup	all-purpose flour	175 mL
1/2 cup	cocoa	125 mL
1 tsp	baking powder	5 mL

1. Make the filling: In a food processor or in a bowl with an electric mixer, beat together cream cheese, sugar, milk and vanilla until smooth. Set aside.

2. Make the cake: In a large bowl, whisk together brown sugar, sour cream, oil, whole egg and egg white. In a separate bowl, stir together flour, cocoa and baking powder. Add liquid ingredients to dry, blending just until mixed.

3. Pour half the cake batter into prepared pan. Spoon filling on top; spread with a wet knife. Pour remaining batter into pan. Bake 20 to 25 minutes or until just barely loose at the center.

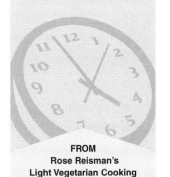

FROM
Rose Reisman's
Light Vegetarian Cooking

Fried Pineapple

Serves 4

Here's one for those occasions when you're short of time but still feel like a good dessert. With staples such as sugar, unsalted butter, good raisins and bittersweet chocolate in your larder, all you need from the store is a ripe pineapple, and then 10 minutes of quick and easy work.

1	ripe pineapple	1
2 tbsp	sugar	25 mL
2 tbsp	unsalted butter	25 mL
2 tbsp	sultana raisins	25 mL
1 oz	bittersweet chocolate, shaved	25 g
4	sprigs fresh mint	4

1. With a sharp knife cut off top half of the pineapple, reserving it for another use. Remove rind from the bottom (sweeter) half and slice the pineapple into 4 rounds, each 1/2 inch (1 cm) thick. Spread sugar on a plate and dredge the pineapple slices in the sugar.

2. In a large frying pan, melt butter over high heat until foaming. Add the dredged pineapple slices and fry for 2 minutes. Flip the slices and spread raisins around them; fry for another 2 to 3 minutes until the pineapple has browned and the raisins are swollen. Remove from heat and transfer one pineapple slice to each of the 4 dessert plates, flipping them so the more attractively browned side faces upward. Spoon some raisins onto each plate and top with a bit of the sauce from the pan. Garnish with chocolate shavings and mint. Serve immediately.

FROM
The New Vegetarian Gourmet
by Byron Ayanoglu

Candied Ginger and Strawberry Parfait

Serves 6

Frozen strawberries can be used if fresh ones are out of season. Be sure to check sweetness before adding honey as some frozen berries may already have sugar added.

•

Candied ginger is usually sold in a jar with syrup, but we have seen it in semi-dried form, coated in sugar. If that's the kind you're using, substitute ginger juice and honey for the syrup. To make ginger juice: In a food processor or chopper, purée 8 thick slices of ginger root and 1 tbsp (15 mL) water. Extract juice by pushing pulp through a very fine sieve.

2 tbsp	minced candied ginger	25 mL
1 tsp	ginger juice (see note at left)	5 mL
1 tbsp	syrup from candied ginger	15 mL
	or 1 tbsp (15 mL) ginger juice, sweetened with 1 tsp (5 mL) honey	
2 cups	sliced strawberries	500 mL
	Maple syrup, to taste	
2 cups	vanilla ice cream	500 mL
1 cup	whipped cream	250 mL

1. In a bowl combine ginger, ginger juice, syrup and strawberries; mix well. Adjust sweetness with maple syrup and set aside to marinate for 20 minutes.

2. To serve: Place about 2 tbsp (25 mL) strawberry mixture in the bottom of a parfait glass. Add 2 tbsp (25 mL) ice cream; repeat layers until parfait glass is filled. Top with a dollop of whipped cream and serve immediately.

FROM
New World Chinese Cooking
by Bill Jones and Stephen Wong

Makes 24 bars

Peanut butter fans will love these no-bake bars. They're a breeze to make and taste so much better than expensive packaged snack bars sold in supermarkets. They are a nice change of pace from that other popular snack for kids — Rice Krispie squares.

TIP

Wrap bars individually in plastic wrap and freeze.Then, when making school lunches, just pop a pre-wrapped bar into each lunch bag.

FROM
The Comfort Food Cookbook
by Johanna Burkhard

Peanutty Cereal Snacking Bars

13- BY 9-INCH (3.5 L) BAKING PAN, GREASED

1 cup	smooth or chunky peanut butter (regular or light)	250 mL
2/3 cup	honey *or* golden corn syrup	150 mL
4 cups	toasted rice cereal	1 L
2 cups	muesli–type cereal with fruit and nuts	500 mL

1. In a large saucepan, combine the peanut butter and honey; cook over medium heat, stirring constantly, until smooth. (Or place in a large glass bowl and microwave at High for 2 minutes, or until smooth, stirring once.)

2. Fold in cereal until evenly coated. Press firmly into the prepared baking pan. Let cool; cut into 3- by 1 1/2-inch (8 by 4 cm) bars.

Baked Wontons Stuffed with Apples and Cinnamon

Serves 4

These tasty treats (which can also be made with pears, bananas, pineapple, blueberries or raspberries) are virtually fat-free, simple to make and cook quickly.

•

Be sure to chop the fruit finely; otherwise, the wonton wrappers won't fit together properly.

PREHEAT OVEN TO 350° F (180° C)

2	apples, peeled and finely diced	1
2 tbsp	brown sugar	25 mL
1/2 tsp	ground cinnamon	2 mL
12	round wonton wrappers	12
1	egg, beaten	1
	Granulated sugar for garnish	

1. In a small bowl, combine the apples, brown sugar and cinnamon; mix thoroughly.

2. On a clean flat surface, lay out 6 wonton wrappers. Brush with the beaten egg. Place 1 heaping tbsp (15 to 17 mL) of the apple mixture on each wrapper. Lay a second wrapper on top of the mixture and, using your fingertips, press lightly to remove the trapped air. Press the edges together to seal. Brush with egg and sprinkle sugar on top.

3. Bake in the preheated oven 10 to 12 minutes or until golden. Remove from the oven and dust with additional sugar, if desired. Serve warm.

FROM
New World Chinese Cooking
by Bill Jones and Stephen Wong

Index

A

Anchovy fillets, Piedmont
  peppers, 63
Antipasto nibblers, 20
Appetizers:
  antipasto nibblers, 20
  Brie-stuffed mushrooms, 9
  crab and corn pancakes, 10
  pesto shrimp tortilla pizzas,
    19
  ricotta and smoked salmon
    tortilla bites, 14
  shrimp and snow pea tidbits,
    15
  Tuscan-style garlic tomato
    bread, 16
Apple pie, 77
Artichokes:
  about, 30
  salad, 30
Asparagus:
  red pepper and cheese
    phyllo roll, 69
  rotini Alfredo with red
    pepper and, 54
Avocado and bean dip, 12

B

Banana blueberry muffins, 79
Bean dip, 12
Beans. *See* Black beans; Kidney
  beans; Navy beans; Pinto
  beans
Beef:
  steak paprikash, 44
  Thai-style salad, 32
  Vietnamese-style noodle
    soup, 24
Bitter greens:
  with balsamic vinegar, 57
  with paprika, 8

Black beans:
  corn and leek frittata, 38
  quesadillas, 73
  salsa, 50
Blueberry banana muffins, 79
Bread, Tuscan-style garlic
  tomato, 16
Brie cheese:
  chicken stuffed with, 40
  mushrooms stuffed with, 9
Broccoli:
  and cheese chowder, 25
  with jalapeno peppers, 64
  rotini Alfredo with red
    pepper and, 54
Brownies:
  cream cheese-filled, 86
  mocha, 85
Bruschetta, 16
Burgers, Italian-style, 43

C

Candied ginger:
  about, 90
  and strawberry parfait, 90
Carrots, lemon-glazed, 58
Cauliflower, and white bean
  soup, 26
Cereal, snacking bars, 91
Cheddar broccoli chowder, 25
Cheese:
  antipasto nibblers, 20
  eggplant with roasted red
    peppers and, 72
  macaroni and, 45
  mushrooms stuffed with, 70
  and red pepper stuffed
    potatoes, 59
  and salsa quesadillas, 73
  See also Brie cheese;
    Cheddar; Feta cheese

Cheeseburgers, Italian-style, 43
Chicken:
  with fig and orange sauce,
    36
  grilled Indian-style, 35
  with lemon sauce on red
    peppers and snow peas, 37
  pita sandwiches, 7
  stuffed with Brie cheese, 40
  Thai-style salad, 32
Chinese-style, lemon chicken
  with peppers and snow peas,
    37
Chocolate fondue, 84
Chowder:
  cheese and broccoli, 25
  See also Soups
Corn:
  with beef and rice noodles,
    41
  black bean and leek frittata,
    38
  and crab pancakes, 10
  ramen noodle soup with
    tomato broth and, 27
Crab meat, and corn pancakes,
  10
Cream cheese:
  -filled brownies, 86
  icing, 85

D

Dandelion greens, with
  paprika, 8
Dips, bean, 12
Dressings:
  mustard, 29
  orange, 32

E

Eggplant, with cheese and roasted red peppers, 72
Eggs, black bean, corn and leek frittata, 38

F

Feta cheese, rice with black olives and, 60
Fett'unta, 16
Fig and orange sauce, 36
Fondue, chocolate, 84
Fool, lemon, 80
Four-cheese macaroni, 45
Frittata, black bean, corn and leek, 38

G

Ginger. *See* Candied ginger
Gnocchi, minestrone with, 23
Greek-style, chicken pitas, 7
Green beans:
   with cashews, 67
   with sesame sauce, 71
   and tomato salad, 29
Guacamole, and bean dip, 12

H

Halibut, with lemon-oregano pesto, 46

I

Icing, cream cheese, 85
Indian-style, grilled chicken, 35
Italian-style, cheeseburgers, 43

J

Jalapeno broccoli, 64

K

Kidney beans, and cauliflower soup, 26

L

Lamb, Vietnamese-style noodle soup, 24
Leeks, black bean and corn frittata, 38
Lemon:
   fool with berries, 80
   -glazed carrots, 58
   poppy seed squares, 78
Linguine, with caramelized onions and tomato, 53

M

Macaroni and cheese, 45
Mango coriander salsa, 49
Minestrone, 23
Mocha brownies, 85
Muffins, blueberry banana, 79
Mushrooms:
   Brie-stuffed, 9
   and the stems, 9
   stuffed with cheese, 70
   veal paprikash, 44

N

Navy beans, and cauliflower soup, 26
Noodles, Vietnamese-style beef soup, 24

O

Omelette, black bean, corn and leek frittata, 38
Orange:
   dressing, 32
   and fig sauce, 36

P

Pancakes, crab and corn, 10
Parfait, ginger and strawberry, 90
Pasta:
   Alfredo with asparagus and red peppers, 54
   with beef and corn, 41

Pasta (continued):
   with caramelized onions and tomato, 53
Peanut butter, cereal snacking bars, 91
Pears, baked, 83
Pesto:
   lemon-oregano with salmon, 46
   shrimp tortilla pizzas, 19
Phyllo rolls, asparagus, red pepper and cheese, 69
Piecrust, 77
Piedmont peppers, 63
Pineapple, fried, 89
Pinto beans:
   dip, 12
   quesadillas, 73
Pita, Greek chicken, 7
Pizzas, pesto shrimp, 19
Pork:
   scallopini,
      with lemon sauce on red peppers and snow peas, 37
      stuffed with Brie cheese, 40
   Thai-style salad, 32
   Vietnamese-style noodle soup, 24
Potatoes:
   herbed, 74
   stuffed with cheese and red pepper, 59

Q

Quesadillas, salsa, 73

R

Ramen noodle soup with tomato and corn broth, 27
Rapini:
   with balsamic vinegar, 57
   with paprika, 8
Ravioli, minestrone with, 23

Red peppers:
  asparagus and cheese phyllo
    roll, 69
  with eggplant and cheese, 72
  lemon chicken with snow
    peas and, 37
  Piedmont-style, 63
  potatoes stuffed with cheese
    and, 59
  See also Sweet peppers
Refried beans, dip, 12
Rice, with feta cheese and
  black olives, 60
Rice noodles, with beef and
  corn, 41
Ricotta and smoked salmon
  tortilla bites, 14
Roasted garlic sweet pepper
  strips, 65
Rotini, Alfredo with asparagus
  and red peppers, 54

S

Salads:
  artichoke, 30
  beef Thai-style, 32
  green bean and tomato, 29
Salmon:
  with lemon-oregano pesto,
    46
  over white-and-black bean
    salsa, 50
  See also Smoked salmon
Salsa:
  mango coriander, 49
  quesadillas, 73
  white-and-black bean, 50
Sandwiches, Greek chicken
  pita, 7
Sauces:
  fig and orange, 36
  sesame, 71
  sweet-and-sour, 10
Scallops, and snow pea tidbits,
  15
Sesame sauce, 71

Shark, with mango coriander
  salsa, 49
Shrimp:
  pesto tortilla pizzas, 19
  and snow pea tidbits, 15
Smoked salmon tortilla bites,
  14
Snacking bars, 91
Snow peas:
  lemon chicken with red
    peppers and, 37
  with sesame sauce, 71
  and shrimp tidbits, 15
Soups:
  cauliflower and white bean,
    26
  minestrone, 23
  ramen noodle with tomato
    and corn broth, 27
  Vietnamese-style beef
    noodle, 24
  See also Chowder
Spinach, minestrone with, 23
Squares, lemon poppy seed, 78
Strawberry and ginger parfait,
  90
Sugar snap peas, with sesame
  sauce, 71
Sweet peppers:
  roasted garlic, 65
  See also Red peppers
Sweet-and-sour sauce, 10
Swordfish:
  with lemon-oregano pesto, 46
  with mango coriander salsa,
    49
  over white-and-black bean
    salsa, 50

T

Thai-style, beef salad, 32
Tomatoes, and green bean
  salad, 29
Tortellini minestrone with
  spinach, 23

Tortillas:
  pesto shrimp, 19
  quesadillas, 73
  ricotta and smoked salmon
    bites, 14
Tuna:
  with lemon-oregano pesto,
    46
  with mango coriander salsa,
    49
  over white-and-black bean
    salsa, 50
Turkey scallopini:
  with lemon sauce on red
    peppers and snow peas, 37
  stuffed with Brie cheese, 40
Tuscan-style garlic tomato
  bread, 16

V

Veal:
  paprikash, 44
  scallopini,
    with lemon sauce on red
      peppers and snow peas,
      37
    stuffed with Brie cheese,
      40
Vietnamese-style beef noodle
  soup, 24

W

White navy beans, salsa, 50
Wontons stuffed with apples,
  92

Z

Zabaglione, 83

More of your favorite recipes

Robert Rose's Favorite
BEEF · PORK & LAMB
RECIPES SELECTED FROM BYRON AYANOGLU · JOHANNA BURKHARD · ANDREW CHASE
CINDA CHAVICH · BILL JONES · ROSE REISMAN · KATHLEEN SLOAN · STEPHEN WONG
ISBN 0-7788-0007-5

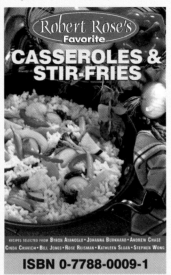

Robert Rose's Favorite
CASSEROLES & STIR-FRIES
RECIPES SELECTED FROM BYRON AYANOGLU · JOHANNA BURKHARD · ANDREW CHASE
CINDA CHAVICH · BILL JONES · ROSE REISMAN · KATHLEEN SLOAN · STEPHEN WONG
ISBN 0-7788-0009-1

Robert Rose's Favorite
MEATLESS MEALS
RECIPES SELECTED FROM BYRON AYANOGLU · JOHANNA BURKHARD
ANDREW CHASE · BILL JONES · ROSE REISMAN · STEPHEN WONG
ISBN 1-896503-67-5

Robert Rose's Favorite
PASTA
RECIPES SELECTED FROM BYRON AYANOGLU · JOHANNA BURKHARD
ANDREW CHASE · BILL JONES · ROSE REISMAN · STEPHEN WONG
ISBN 1-896503-74-8

Robert Rose's Favorite
LIGHT DESSERTS
ISBN 1-896503-72-1

Robert Rose's Favorite
COOKIES CAKES & PIES
RECIPES SELECTED FROM BYRON AYANOGLU · JOHANNA BURKHARD
ANDREW CHASE · BILL JONES · ROSE REISMAN · STEPHEN WONG
ISBN 1-896503-71-3

Robert Rose's Favorite
SNACKS · SALADS & APPETIZERS
RECIPES SELECTED FROM BYRON AYANOGLU · JOHANNA BURKHARD
ANDREW CHASE · BILL JONES · ROSE REISMAN · STEPHEN WONG
ISBN 1-896503-51-9

Robert Rose's Favorite
SOUPS & STEWS
RECIPES SELECTED FROM BYRON AYANOGLU · JOHANNA BURKHARD
ANDREW CHASE · BILL JONES · ROSE REISMAN · STEPHEN WONG
ISBN 1-896503-69-1

Robert Rose's Favorite
CHICKEN
RECIPES SELECTED FROM BYRON AYANOGLU · JOHANNA BURKHARD
ANDREW CHASE · BILL JONES · ROSE REISMAN · STEPHEN WONG
ISBN 1-896503-53-5